Copyright © 2018 Roy Landers and Rainbow Publishing Company. All rights reserved.

No portion of this publication may be reprinted or reproduced in any way without the author's written permission. A reproduction of even a single page is a violation of United States and international copyright law. Violators of this agreement will be prosecuted to the fullest extent of the law.

This publication is designed to provide accurate and authoritative information regarding the subject matter covered. It is sold with the understanding that the publisher is not engaged in rendering legal, accounting, or other professional services. If legal advice or other expert assistance is required, the services of a competent professional person should be sought.

For more information, contact:

Roy Landers
Rainbow Publishing Company
10679 Westview Parkway

San Diego, CA 92126

Discounts are available for bulk purchases.
Email: info@roylanders.com

Acknowledgements

This book is the result of a long-traveled journey that continues. After many starts and stops it is finally complete in one sense but the theme -negotiation-continues. I want to thank and recognize so many people that in so many ways helped me to create this publication.

They encouraged me when I was going through episodes of frustration, sometimes depression and bouts of when I just didn't want to do anything. What I have come to realize is they negotiated me through the process as I put together piece by piece the thing that I so desperately wanted to share with the world and what I've learned over many years. What I learned is that the ability to negotiate well is crucial to success.

To all those who have stood by me along the way I give a heartfelt thank you.

To my wife, Princetta, who exercised the greatest patience and encouragement and helped me brave through the darkest of times and loved me through it all, I thank you from the bottom of my heart. To my daughter Natasha who has always had my back no matter what through thick and thin and to my granddaughter Sasha, who is my inspiration, and who also helped me dust off and hone the negotiation techniques I share in this book through her challenges and questioning of me and never giving up when I've told her NO so many times. She is the epitome of an example of how to get past NO and get to YES. Thank you, Sasha.

To my son, Roy Jr. who always had a smile and a way of making me laugh and often forced me to relax and just watch a movie with him to chill. Those times were precious. He has departed and gone on to glory, but his spirit is still strong with me and always will be.

Thank you to my Son-In-Law, Stephen Reese, for being a positive part of my family, a great husband and blessing to my daughter, Natasha, and for being part of the blessing from God in producing Sasha, my granddaughter, who is the sunshine of my latter years.

Thanks to all the family and friends who have encouraged me and supported me through the ups and downs of my career and professional life. You too, were part of the journey

Finally, I thank my mother Willie Mae Dowdy, who has gone on to be with the Lord, for the example she set for me and my sisters and brothers. Although a woman with only a sixth-grade education, she was wise and as solid as a rock. She would not allow her children to give up and the word can't was not allowed to be part of our vocabulary.

She laid the foundation for what I've become, who I am and where I will go. Thank you, mom.

Contents

Introduction 1

Chapter 1 Understanding human motivation and emotions - the foundation for successful negotiations 5

Chapter 2 The power of perception. Whatever is perceived is believed. 13

Chapter 3 Never negotiate without first being informed. Gather information before you go. 17

Chapter 4 Use reluctance to move negotiations forward 34

Chapter 5 How to use time as a negotiating ally. 40

Chapter 6 Ask and you shall receive. Ask for more than you expect to get 44

Chapter 7 Never accept the first offer made. It's not the real deal. 49

Chapter 8 Watch out for these two negotiation traps 53

Chapter 9 What to do with the "I don't have authority" negotiation response 60

Chapter 10 You'll have to do better than that! The magical phrase that gets amazing results. 67

Chapter 11 In negotiations you get by giving, but don't give until you create a return from the other side. 72

Chapter 12 Use the flinch or wince technique (Shock and awe negotiating) 77

Chapter 13 Body language – the truth teller in negotiations. 84

Chapter 14 What not to do in negotiations. Don't set yourself up for failure 95

Chapter 15 Avoiding negotiation sleaze and squeeze – Unethical actions by the other side and how to deal with them. 100

Chapter 16 Biblical principles for negotiation success. 109

Chapter 17 If it's not enough, don't be afraid to ask for more. 122

Chapter 18 Getting the deal on paper. Beware of the pitfalls 128

Chapter 19 Negotiation Review Guidelines.................................. 136

CONCLUSION 143

ABOUT THE AUTHOR 144

Introduction

Negotiation is the process of communicating wants and desires between one person and another to reach the ultimate goal of getting what the person, company, government or country wants. It doesn't matter whether it's on a small scale of just getting what is desired for one person or a whole nation, negotiation principles apply across the board.

Every person wants, needs or desires something. How to get those things is more difficult for some than others and the difference between them is always the ability to negotiate.

Some people have more natural ability to negotiate or persuade and get what they want than others, but the bottom line is that anyone can learn the basic skills of negotiation and how to apply those principles to change their life, create a better future, get a job, win the love and affection of the person they want to be with, build a business, make a sale or whatever the case might be.

Human beings are all the same when it comes to negotiation. It does not matter what race, culture or creed one is from. We all, as human beings, share the same wants, needs and desires and we all react to the same emotional stimulus that makes us come to decisions and conclusions whether good or bad.

Negotiation is based on these principles and when the fundamentals are mastered you can become a competent negotiator the same as an individual who has mastered the art of any martial art sport, an actor's part in a movie script or whatever it might be.

One thing to always remember in any negotiation, no matter how small or large the stakes, is a basic concept that I learned early on while gaining experience as a negotiator. I like to compare it with the concept of listening to a radio station on an FM frequency. Music, news and entertainment have affects and effects generally on every person. Mostly everyone is interested in being informed and entertained so people listen to radio, watch television, read the newspaper, a magazine or just google it to stay informed.

We tune in to a particular media outlet or station because it is our favorite or because we know that particular source provides us with all the need for obtaining the news, entertainment or music we want. Radio is a huge influencer and people have their favorite station to tune in to and make that station the one they listen to more than any other.

Similarly, in negotiations there is also a "station", so to speak, that every person tunes in to everyday of their lives. Every day when a person wakes up they tune in to this station and we, as human beings, listen to the same station every day. Its call letters are WIIFM. It is an FM frequency that we keep open and never get enough of listening to.

The WIIFM is an acronym for <u>W</u>hat's <u>I</u>n <u>I</u>t <u>F</u>or <u>M</u>e. Just think about that for a moment. WIIFM, what's in it for me? Isn't that the thing that's in the back of your mind whenever you are negotiating or whenever someone is trying to convince or persuade you to do something, not to do something or buy something? Negotiations can be simple or complex, but the bottom line is always that station WIIFM is being broadcast loud and clear inside the heads and hearts of those involvedin the negotiating process.

Those involved in the negotiation are consciously and unconsciously saying to themselves (What's in it for me? WIIFM) each time the other side makes a move or countermove.

Just keeping this simple concept in mind and applying the negotiation principles outlined in this book will take you a very long way in mastering negotiation skills and getting what you want.

You already have natural skills to negotiate. You were born with them. In fact, you were a much better negotiator when you were a small child than you likely are now. If you doubt it just think about this. Have you ever seen how small children are masters at negotiating to get what they want?

They haven't been to school, they haven't been exposed to studied tactics and techniques of how to get what you want, they don't have a regimen that they follow that has been taught by a guru, but they are master negotiators. They instinctively know how to read parents and anyone who they encounter and want something from. They are experts when it comes to calling forth the right emotion at the right time to persuade or dissuade the opponent and they are relentless when it comes to staying focused and on track to reach their goal.

They never get discouraged when they are told no. They will ask again and again as if they don't even understand what the word no means. They will even wait and come back from a different angle and ask again. Their attitude is always one of expectancy of getting what they want so their body language is congruent with their expectations.

You can see it in their little eyes, their expression and a smile. Are you getting the clue here? They will wear you down over a period of time and usually the parent or adult will give in not realizing that the child knew all along that if he or she just kept going toward the goal of what was wanted eventually they would get it.

God gives children natural abilities to negotiate and they use it without fear of being told no because they know that it's likely just temporary. With an expectation of success and with a dogged persistence children instinctively know how to get what they want. Somewhere along the way as human beings grow up these natural traits are subdued and pushed deep inside us to the point where we forget them and fear and doubt creeps in and takes us hostage. We lose the ability to negotiate. We become fearful of the word "no". We even conjure up things in our mind that hinders our negotiation process that in most instances never even come up in the negotiation.

This book is designed to assist in the rebirth of those natural skills we were born with and to provide a roadmap to hone and sharpen those skills so you can be confident when negotiating for whatever it is you might be involved in. Applying the strategies, tactics and techniques in this book will help you become a skillful negotiator.

Chapter One

Understanding Human Motivation and Emotions - the Foundation for Successful Negotiations.

Human beings are emotional creatures and even though we might not admit it, we make decisions based on our emotions. Emotions are so strong that they over shadow logic. Logic might say to a young man that a particular car shouldn't be purchased just yet because his budget just won't support the extra payment.

However, the emotional feeling and need to be in the in-crowd, to have a car like or better than a rival for a young woman's affection and attention and a host of other things will override the logic and that car will be purchased. Later on logic will be used to justify the purchase of the car that was bought purely based on emotion.

For instance, logic will rationalize it was worth the purchase and creation of the car debt because now I have a better chance to compete for the young woman's attention. It doesn't matter that there may have been a number of other ways to accomplish this goal. Emotions got in the way and logic went out the window.

This is the way most negotiations are handled too, particularly when it comes to one on one negotiation and the basic negotiations of everyday life. If you understand what basic emotions all humans are driven by you instantly become a better negotiator than the average person you will meet or encounter whenever you are involved in negotiating your way to get what you want.

If you know the emotional triggers of the human psychic and learn how to use them you can negotiate anything to your advantage.

Several studies have proven that there are basic emotions that drive our decision making process. Negotiation success is largely based upon the science of influence - what we as human beings perceive, feel, think or fear. One of the most well-known and applied studies of influence and understanding of how people make decisions is contained in Robert Cialdini's book Influence.

He identifies six basic emotional triggers that govern just about all decisional making processes. He refers to them as Reciprocity, Commitment and Consistency, Social Proof, Liking, Authority and Scarcity. Dr. Cialdini refers to these emotional triggers as "weapons of influence". Indeed they are weapons and as I share with you my experience and application of these principles in this book it will be revealed how these "weapons of influence" are the core tools for powerful negotiation tactics and techniques.

Briefly, the concept of reciprocity is based upon the natural and very strong tendency to respond in kind to someone when they give you something that is perceived as value to you. No matter what it is or who the person is there is just something that is innately within a human being that compels them to have a feeling (emotion) to give back to the person or entity that gave that person something.

Have you ever felt like you just need to give someone something when they've bestowed a gift on you? Your natural instinct is to want to respond. In fact, if you don't give back to the person who gave you the gift there is often a twinge of guilt. When negotiating the concept of giving should be kept in mind.

If you give the right gift, make the right concession, stroke the right emotion, the person on the other side is automatically put into an emotional state of thinking the need to reciprocate in like manner.

Similarly, the concept of social proof is a very strong negotiating tactic. Social proof is nothing more than seeing what others are doing or things other people have and wanting to blend in and have the same thing, belong to the same crowd or club or own the same or similar car. It gives the sense that you belong. It creates comfort, yet another strong emotion.

Remember the young man vying for the affection and attention of the young woman? He purchased the car to compete with his rival and belong to the club so to speak. He wanted to prove he was just as good, acceptable or perhaps better than the competition. That's call social proof.

It happens all the time and is used by corporations and businesses to influence sales. We buy clothes because we want to look like the latest model. Men, in particular, and many women, purchase a certain brand of tennis or sport shoe because they want to be like "Mike" – Michael Jordan, Kobe Bryant, LeBron James etc. They want to be as close to being like them as possible. That's social proof.

Authority is one of the emotional triggers that I have used extensively throughout my career and it has made me a lot of money. People are conditioned to respond to authority figures. Think about it. What do you think of when you see a police officer nearby or a highway patrol car cruising up behind you? You immediately look down at your speedometer or make sure you come to a full stop at the stop sign.

You wouldn't give it a second thought if it was just another ordinary citizen driving a car or looking at you as you just ran that stop light. Authority is very powerful. As an attorney and former Pro Tem Judge that sat in the court room and made numerous decisions affecting the lives of people, I make sure that these titles and experiences are somehow made aware to the person or persons that I am engaged in negotiations with. Why, because these are authority positions and they give me an edge. That's what you're looking for in any negotiation, an edge.

Even the way you dress can create an authority perception that gives you an edge. For instance, generally speaking, a man in a well-fitting suit and polished shoes or a woman with a very nice dress and groomed the best she can be will be more impressive in negotiating than someone who is not "dressed for the occasion". It's just the way it is.

Doctors and nurses in uniform are given a great deal of respect and will be listened too because they come across as authority figures. Without saying a word just their appearance creates an environment of power, knowledge and control. Compliance from a person becomes much easier if you are perceived as an authority. I hope you are getting this.

When negotiating find a way to present yourself as an authority figure. You don't have to have a string of degrees behind your name nor do you have to be the best dressed person in the world. You can be an authority figure by creating a brochure about the subject matter that you are negotiating about.

Providing information that solves a problem that the other side is experiencing makes you the expert. You can establish your authority by learning from other sources and when you come to the negotiating table you are armed with material and facts that support your position. That gives you authority.

Liking is another huge negotiating influence. Human beings just can't help themselves. We like doing business with people we like - plain and simple. If you like someone, whether you just met them or have known them for a long period of time, you are more apt to do business with them, to buy from them or give them what they ask for than you are to someone who you don't like or have no affinity for. Never forget this concept in negotiation. In every negotiation you should strive to attain some level of likeability. That does not mean you are seeking to have that person become your friend. It does mean you need to create a measure of rapport.

Always seek to set a stage of non-confrontation before the start of any negotiation.

What you say in the first few moments of a negotiation usually sets the environment of the negotiation. The other person quickly gets a feel for whether you are working for a win-win solution, or whether you're a tough negotiator who is out for everything they can get.

Many people have the mistaken idea or understanding that effective negotiation means being very confrontational and sending a strong message of how big and bad they are at the beginning of negotiation.

Unfortunately, lawyers are notorious for this type of negotiation tactic. They send that white envelope in the mail with black raised lettering in the top left hand corner, many of them with a list of names in the firm that you can't even pronounce, and you think, "Oh, no! What is it this time?" You open the letter and what's the first thing they do? They start off with a threat and tell you what bad consequences will follow if you don't do this or that.

Think about that for a moment. If that's the way negotiations start where will they usually go after that? Yes, you guessed it, downhill in a hurry. It's much better to always seek to establish an atmosphere of mutual respect at the outset of the negotiations. It is human nature to push back whenever one is being pushed no matter what the odds are on the other side.

If the other person takes a position with which you totally disagree don't argue. Arguing always intensifies the other person's desire to prove they are right. You're much better off to agree with the other person initially and then turn it around using what is known as the Feel, Felt, Found technique.

Respond with, "I understand exactly how you feel about that. Many other people have felt exactly the same way as you do right now". Now you have diffused that competitive spirit. You're not arguing with them, you're agreeing with them. You have emphasized and empathized with them. This takes their guard down. Then you continue with, "but you know most people have found when they know all of the facts they usually have a different viewpoint." This sets the stage for you to show your position without being confrontational.

Let's look at some examples:

- You're selling something, and the other person says, "Your price is way too high." If you argue with him, he has a personal stake in proving you wrong and him being right. Instead, you say, "I understand exactly how you feel about that. Many other people have felt exactly the same way as you do when they first hear the price. When they take a closer look at what we offer, however, they have always found that we offer the best value in the marketplace."

- You're applying for a job, and the human resources director says, "I don't think you have enough experience in this field." If you respond with, "I've handled much tougher jobs than this in the past," it may come across as, "I'm right and you're wrong." It's just going to force the interviewer to defend the position already taken. Instead, say, "I understand exactly how you feel about that. Many other people would feel exactly the same way as you do right now. However, there are some remarkable similarities between the work I've been doing and what you're looking for that is not immediately apparent. Let me tell you what they are."

- If the other person says, "I don't believe in buying from off-shore suppliers. I think we should keep the jobs in this country," the more you argue the more you'll force him into defending his position. Instead, say, "I understand exactly how you feel about that, because these days many other people feel exactly the same way as you do. But do you know what we have found? Since we have been having the initial assembly done in Mexico, we have actually been able to increase our American work force by more than 42 percent and this is why . . ."

So instead of arguing up front, which creates confrontational negotiation, get in the habit of agreeing and then turning it around.

At my seminars, I sometimes ask a person in the front row to stand. As I hold my two hands out, with my palms facing toward the person

I've asked to stand, I ask him or her to place their hands against mine. Having done that and without saying another word, I gently start to push against them. Automatically, without any instruction, instinctively they always begin to push back. It's just human nature, most people shove back when you shove them. Similarly, when you argue with someone, it automatically makes them want to argue back.

The other great thing about Feel, Felt, Found is that it gives you time to think. Sometimes something will come up in a negotiation that you weren't expecting. You haven't heard anything like this before. It shocks you. You don't know what to say, but if you have Feel, Felt, Found in the back of your mind, you can say, "I understand exactly how you feel about that. Many other people have felt exactly the same way. However, I have always found . . ." By the time you get there, you'll have thought of something to say.

Similarly, you sometimes catch other people at a bad moment. You may be a salesperson who is calling to get an appointment and the person says to you, "I don't have any more time to waste talking to you because it seems only to be self-serving to you." You calmly say, "I understand exactly how you feel about that. Many other people have felt exactly the same way. However . . ." By the time you get there you will have recovered your composure and will know exactly what to say. If you practice this technique and make it one of the tools in your negotiation box, it will help you be successful in your negotiation attempts.

Here's the reason this particular negotiating technique is so powerful. It uses empathy to draw the other person in and makes it natural for him or her to let their guard down a bit. Showing empathy is a powerful way to gain leverage in any negotiation.

Empathy is the psychological identification with or vicarious experiencing of the feelings, thoughts, or attitudes of another. It is the power of understanding and imaginatively entering into another person's feelings. In other words, put yourself in the shoes and position of the other person, company, entity, government etc. Imagine you are them and do your best to feel what they are feeling, see things the way they are seeing them, hear things how they might be hearing them and reacting to what is happening.

If you do this, you then get an immediate sense of where they are coming from and can identify with what they are likely, at that very moment, experiencing and enter into their feelings. You then know how best to react and help them move to the next point in the negotiation.

This is done by, once again, first acknowledging how they feel. You can then relate their feelings to how others have felt in the same circumstances and suggest that others when they found what you are suggesting benefited them changed their position and the outcome was more favorable to them. The feel, felt found technique can be a game changer in negotiations. Master it and success in getting what you want will follow.

Key points to remember:

- Negotiation is an emotional exercise. It is not a logical exchange.
- Don't argue with people in the early stages of the negotiation because it creates confrontation.
- Use the Feel, Felt, Found technique to turn the hostility around.
- Having Feel, Felt, Found in the back of your mind gives you time to think when the other side throws some unexpected hostility or roadblock in your way.
- Use empathy to break down the other side's barriers.

Chapter Two

The Power of Perception. Whatever Is Perceived Is Believed.

What most people see or perceive forms their views and what they believe ultimately governs how they will make a choice one way or the other. Right or wrong that's just the way human beings are wired. We are more visually affected than by any other of our senses. There is something to the cliché that human beings use such as "I see your point", "I can't see that happening" or "show me". There is even long standing folklore regarding the state of Missouri. It's called the show me state. What people see they are apt to believe.

Never under estimate the power of perception. It can make or break a negotiation in your favor. A person's perception is reality to that individual. Therefore, when you are seeking to negotiate with someone seek to understand how they perceive things. If you know you don't have the power controlled position going into a negotiation find a way to make it appear that you do have that power. It will work the same as if you had the power.

I learned early in my life the power of perception and how to use it. I recall an instant when I was a young sailor walking along the road and a car full of fellows apparently looking for a brawl after a night of drinking accosted me on the street. They stopped the car and just for the heck of it, I suppose, intended to physically harm me. They were all larger and likely stronger, but I had learned a thing or two about creating a tough image. They stopped and yelled at me and stopped the car they were riding in. I knew I had to think very quickly or I would be on the receiving end of a brutal beating.

During that period of time there were still very sensitive issues of race between African Americans and whites, even in the military. There was also a myth that existed at the time that African American males, in particular, were notorious for carrying knifes and/or razors and they would violently cut an opponent in a physical encounter. Knowing these facts (really the perception) as I was approached by three menacing white males I stood my ground and reached inside my pocket as if I was pulling out a knife.

I slowly formed my hand as if I had a lethal weapon ready to do substantial damage to at least one if not all of them before the fight would be finished. I even looked at them and told them as they approached me that I had a razor and was just itching to slit somebody's throat. I made a gesture as if I was moving toward them instead of running. At about that time a very strange thing happened.

There was a young woman who was also in the car and she perceived (thought) I indeed had a lethal weapon and yelled "he has a knife. You better get out of there because he will kill one of you". Suddenly it apparently was perceived by those fellows that not only was I unafraid of them but had the power to inflict serious if not deadly injury. They immediately retreated to their car and sped off leaving me trembling and shaking from the incident but realizing the power of creating a perception that, although not true in reality, it was true to them because what they perceived is what they believed. It was a lesson learned and an understanding about the power of perception that I've used hundreds of times since.

I've used it in my law practice to win cases. During one trial where I was questioning a witness, I had a box that I kept retrieving documents from to challenge the witness's untruthful responses. This witness was testifying on behalf of a government entity that I had sued on behalf of a client. I used the documents from the box to discredit the witness in a number of ways.

Sitting in the courtroom was another employee who worked for the same government entity and was watching the whole episode of how I had discredited the government witness. I then called that person as my next witness. As soon as I began to question that witness I asked a question that was crucial for gaining advantage on behalf of my client. The witness hesitated and then gave an answer that was incomplete. I moved toward the box as if I was going to retrieve a document and asked the witness if he wanted to stick with his answer.

He immediately changed his answer and gave an answer that proved the point I was trying to make. The witness even said "you probably have a document in that box that would discredit me anyway." I did not, but I knew he had been watching me question the prior witness and I had used documents from the box to discredit the prior witness.

Because he had witnessed it, this witness perceived that I likely had documents to do the same thing to him. I knew that but, in reality, I had no such document at all. I simply used the power of perception to make it appear that I had such a document. It forced him to testify and give me the information I wanted whereas, he would not have done so otherwise. What a person perceives is what they usually will believe. What they believe is what motivates them to take or refrain from a particular action or to agree or not agree to a particular point of view.

In negotiations, making something appear real is the same as it being real. Use it when you need it to gain the upper hand and close the deal.

The power of perception and reality can be used in a number of ways to give you the upper hand in negotiating.

Key points to remember

Authority figures are powerful. – If you are perceived to have authority and power it's the same as truly having it.

- **Title power** – if you have a title, like doctor, lawyer, engineer or similar learned or experienced title you can use it to influence negotiations.

- **Expertise power** – if you have or can get a certificate, degree or certification in something that is recognized in an acceptable way use that to help you negotiate. We live in a society that honors and respects achievement and paper documents that validate those achievements. This gives you expertise and power if it relates to something you are negotiating about. In many instances just having the experience alone will give you a leg up in

  negotiating.

- **How you perceive it** is how you receive it.

These examples are not exhaustive. Use your imagination and whatever you have to form the kind of perception you want the other side to have of you during a negotiation. Remember, it can be real or perceived to be real. The results are the same.

Chapter Three

Never Negotiate without First Being Informed. Gather Information Before You Go.

As the saying goes, "knowledge is power". However, to be a successful negotiator you must understand that having knowledge is just half of the equation. You must apply the knowledge or it won't accomplish what you would like to achieve. Never go into a negotiation without having as much knowledge about the circumstances concerning the person(s) or entities you are negotiating with as you can.

The more you know the more you can fashion negotiation tactics to move them toward what you ultimately want to accomplish. If you don't have some idea of what the other side wants, how they think or what problems they seek solutions to, your negotiations will be hampered and not nearly as effective as they could be.

Before any negotiation, seek to find out the problems, pain points or pleasure seeking points the other side is looking for answers or solutions to. Fundamentally, negotiations are about providing solutions to problems, removal or avoidance of pain or the acquisition of a pleasurable experience. When you come to the negotiation table with the ability to provide solutions to problems or removing challenges facing the other side or make it clear that you are the answer to what they seek, you are in a powerful position.

Your main job as a negotiator is to find ways and means to enable, enhance or support the opponent to get what they want and, in the process, get all of what you want or as close to all of what you want as possible.

Understand that everything is a negotiation. No matter how small or how insignificant it may be everything is a negotiation. People want things and in return they will give something to get what they want. Companies, states, countries and nations are no different. Find out first what those wants, needs and desires are and construct a way for them to get them and you will be positioned to be a powerful and effective negotiator.

One of the often-cited examples of a great negotiator is former Secretary of State Henry Kissinger. Mr. Kissinger was once asked if he already knew what the Soviets would propose at an upcoming summit meeting. He said, "Oh, absolutely-no question about it. It would be absolutely disastrous for us to go into a negotiation not knowing in advance what the other side was going to propose."

Can you imagine the cost and work that must be put into such an endeavor to know what another nation is thinking or plotting prior to entering into negotiations with it? Millions and possibly billions are spent on espionage, secret and double agents, Central Intelligence (C.I.A) and the National Security Council. However, it is done and the money is spent because the stakes are so high. Our nation has to know as much as possible what any other nation is going to do or is thinking of doing in order to maintain our nation's security and power position in a world that is always steeped in controversy, disagreement and danger.

Here's the point. If governments think it's important enough to spend that kind of money. Doesn't it make sense that you should at least spend a little time to find out more about the other side before going into negotiations? Why do countries send spies into other countries? Why do professional basketball, football and other teams study the replays of their opponents' games? Because knowledge is power and the more knowledge one side is able to accumulate about the other the better chance that side has for victory.

If two countries go to war, the country that has the most intelligence about the other has the advantage. The war on terrorism is a good example. President Barrack Obama made a promise during his first campaign for the U.S. Presidency. He said, if elected, he would capture or kill Osama Ben Laden. It took him a while to do it but in his first term he in fact found out where Ben Laden was hiding and negotiated through various channels to have the Navy Seals take Ben Laden out.

That would have never happened without intelligence or information gathering, gaining knowledge through whatever channels that was necessary, and then coordinating with people inside the hostile country of Pakistan. The knowledge acquired allowed for precision, stealth and completion. It was a consummate negotiated activity that resulted in taking out one of the greatest threats that America has ever faced.

The same was true in the Persian Gulf War that took down Sadam Hussein. U.S. intelligence, through sophisticated methods and strategically placed spies, photographed every roadway, building and mountain area in Baghdad, and were able to completely take out their communication systems in the first few bombing missions.

If two companies are planning to merge, the company that knows the most will usually end up with the better deal. If two salespeople are vying for an account, the salesperson who knows more about the company and its representatives stands a better chance of being selected for the account.

Whether negotiating one on one with an individual, on behalf of a group, company or larger organization, having some or acquiring some information about the other side before you commence negotiations is crucial.

Here's another example, if a male seeks the attention of a female and wants to convince her that he should be given serious consideration and possibly make him her choice it would behoove that male to learn some important facts about her first. What is her favorite color? Watch how she dresses, what family values does she have, who is her favorite celebrity, what perfume does she wear, when is her birthday, etc.

Once this information is known the negotiation process can start with wearing clothes that reflect her favorite color, complementing (not too obvious) about how smartly she dresses, talking positively about the celebrity she adores and perhaps providing an article written on the celebrity –is the light bulb coming on? Are you getting the picture? Negotiations don't just happen. They are studied and then acted upon.

Even shopping is a negotiation. Everyone who has bought a car has experienced the bait and switch tactics of the car salesperson who always says one thing and then has to check with the sales manager before the deal can be sealed. Invariably the sales manager has a twist that is offered instead but it is made to entice you even more and to get you excited. They will tell you to get into the car and say "let's go for a test drive." Once you are in that car you smell the new car scent, you start to feel ownership of the car, you feel the power of the roaring engine, even your mind starts to picture how your friends will ooh and awe about your new car.

This is the car dealership's negotiation tactic. They work your emotions because they know that people fundamentally make decisions based on emotions and then later justify their decisions with logic. You often are trapped and make a decision that you might not have made had you gone into the dealership armed with information and a plan.

Had you first determined the specific type of car you want, the price range you were willing to pay, the limitations of any financing of the deal, the performance information on the car you obtained from consumer reports or the auto manufacturer and developed your walk away mindset before you entered the dealership the results would very likely be different. Better yet, if you have already arranged for financing of your car or can pay cash guess who is in the power position. When the car dealer offers financing you can say I've already arranged for financing and I won't be interested in anything beyond that. What message do you think you just sent?

When you are offered add on items that jack up the price on the car, you are already prepared because you knew those before you came and about how much all of that would cost before you arranged your financing. Your mindset is much more powerful and now you can negotiate from a position of power. If you already know the manufacturers' suggested price, you know it's only a suggestion and subject to negotiation. You know the dealership wants a sale. You have the power to provide them that. What they will do for you is the question.

The more information you have the better you can negotiate and get what you want. Never go into any negotiation without having as much knowledge about the other side's wants needs and desires. You then know their hot buttons and can fashion negotiation tactics to get what you want by showing them the benefit of giving you what you want.

Lastly, you should decide what your walk away point is. If you have determination, courage and power to just walk away from a deal rather than take it to your disadvantage you are in a powerful position. Don't be afraid to walk away. Leave the door open for a later time. This is a powerful tactic to use when you know you have additional time before you really need to make a decision about what it is you're trying to accomplish.

Despite the obvious and important role that information plays in a negotiation, few people spend much time analyzing the other side before starting to negotiate. Even people who wouldn't dream of skiing or scuba diving without first taking lessons will jump into a negotiation that could cost them thousands of dollars or personal failure and disappointment without spending adequate time gathering the information they should have.

What to do when you don't have information on your side.

Rule One: Research and gather as much information as you can about the person, company, group, etc. before you start negotiation.

There is so much information available to assist in any negotiation now that it makes no sense to start any negotiation without being armed with a bundle of information. If you are serious about becoming a skilled negotiator or just need help in engaging in a onetime negotiation, the more information you have before the negotiation the better.

If you have no information at all do some basic research. You'll be surprised at what you can find. The internet is a good place to start to find the information that you need whether it's about a person, place, thing, company, government or whatever. You don't have to go overboard. However, if you choose to you can be as detailed as you want.

Getting information is fairly easy if you know where to look and use the right tools. You can find just about anything you want about anybody or anything by the click of a computer mouse, using a smartphone or a tablet.

It doesn't matter if you are negotiating on a subject that is personal to you and you are negotiating with only one person or you are preparing to negotiate for a job, seeking to close a huge contract, representing a national or international company or even a government entity.

Information gathering tips:

Gathering information before entering into a negotiation is crucial but not that difficult. You don't need to know every intimate detail. Just a few facts about the person, company or group usually will make all the difference in your ability to negotiate for positive results. With all the available information sources accessible now, there really is no excuse for having basic information that you need to help you win in negotiation. Here is a list of places and tools that you can use to obtain information.

- Google Search – Likely, you are already familiar with Google and its giant search engine. Whatever you can think of Google most likely already has it archived somewhere. You just have to know how to use it. Simply type in whatever subject or thought you want to get information on and click the search button.

Google is a monster store of information on just about anything or anyone you can think of. If a person, company, nation, etc. has been on the internet and most assuredly one way or the other most have you can simply go to the google search engine and put in their name.

You might be surprised at what comes up. Birthdays likes and desires, divorces, deaths, bankruptcies and the list goes on and on. Gather this information and sort through it and put it in the best format for you to use in your negotiation.

Google will search the entire World Wide Web and come back with an instant list of everything that relates to your subject. If you want to narrow the search you can put the search term in quotation marks like ("search") and only the items that match that term will be displayed. If you really want to get detailed and become well informed use Google Console. It will literally blow your mind on what you can do to find the things you want and need to help you negotiate to get what you want.

When you use Google Search you can also stroll down to the bottom of the page and Google will give you suggested words and phrases to use to help you with your search.

- Google Trends – If you want to know what the latest and hot topics of the world are or what's happening in a local region or even what a city is buzzing about, Google trends is a good start. It will give you solid information on what is trending now and the demand for the subject you are researching and how long the trend has lasted.

You can search for subjects over the past few days, weeks and even years on how that particular subject has been trending.

Use this data to help you create a powerful negotiating strategy.

- Google People Search - Using Google, you can enter a phone number or email address to find out the owner of that number or email address. You can look for a person and also to get his personal information using Google. The best and easiest way you can start your search on the Web is Google when it comes to getting genuine and sufficient information about somebody. You can check background information, phone numbers, addresses, email addresses, etc by means of Google People Search.

- Google Alerts – if you want to be specific and have google perform information gathering for you, you can go to google alert and create free periodic reports that will tell you every time a person's name has been mentioned on the internet and what they've been doing.

  It also works with companies, products, locations etc. You can even have Google send this to your email account on a daily, weekly, monthly or as it happens basis. So, if you are getting ready for a job interview with a large company you could simply google the information or have google alerts sent to you and gather all the information you need before the negotiation for your new job.

- Whitepages.com– helps you contact, research and verify people. Accordingly, to the website, more than 30 million people per month use its people search engine to get in touch with extended friends and family, research backgrounds and verify if people are who they say they are. There is a free and paid membership.

  The free membership is usually enough to get the basic information that one might need to help in a negotiation process. For a small amount the paid section opens a huge information source.

- Peoplefinders.com – PeopleFinders is a data service that allows you to simply and effectively search for people with confidence and peace of mind. It has a free access application which makes itcost-effective and the quality of information is good and accurate. It also has paid access for a small fee that provides information that doesn't skimp on quality or quantity and gives you the added bonus of unlimited background searches.

- Pipl.com - With the world's largest people search engine, Pipl claims to be the place to find the person behind an email address, social username or phone number. It has over 3 billion listings and connections that allow you to search all social media accounts for information on a person, company or business all in one place.

- Zabasearch.com – ZabaSearch is one of the best and most sought after people search engines. It is commonly used for finding someone's location and contact information online. With ZabaSearch, you will be able to get the telephone numbers and addresses, instant search results with no registration, more residential listings than White Pages Phone Directory, and the finest finder of other people you could ever want.

- Peekyou.com - PeekYou is a useful medium available to people to come across a person you want and get their details. It is a free people search engine that permits you to identify and get in touch with anyone online. With this people search engine, you can discover social links, photos, work history, alumni info, family and more. It permits you to look for usernames across a variety of social networks and it helps you to get instant search results as well.

- Yahoosearch.com

- FacebookPeopleSearch.com

- Refseek – provides a listing of directories and almanacs with free access to information all in one place. This information gathering tool is extremely useful and provides accurate information that can be relied upon. https://www.refseek.com/directory/almanacs.html

- Amazon.com – Although, you might not think of Amazon as a research tool, it is one of the best for determining what's trending, what people are demanding in books and products, what competitors are doing and much more. Going to the website and checking out its best sellers in books, categories and etc. or finding out what the demand for certain items are will reveal a treasure of information. Don't sell this source short in your research.

- Magazines.com – If a subject has any value at all, likely it is covered by a magazine or journal of some sort. By accessing this website one can discover what magazines there are that cover just about any subject. Usually there is free access to some of the back articles or limited access that can be used for research purposes.

  If there is a particular article within a magazine that proves or supports your point you can simply order that particular edition of the magazine and use it to support the position you want to advance.

- Essential government sites – Government information, reports, statistics, articles etc. are powerful in any negotiation. After all, "the government said it." Using this phrase can always be used as support and a factual basis to back up an argument. This is another way of using the power of authority as well. https://www.lifewire.com/essential-government-sites-3482757

- Free Public Records Source – Public records search are documents that local, state and national sources, even international sources have complied. Use this free source of information to help gather information to support your negotiation endeavors.

https://www.lifewire.com/public-records-online-free-3482360

- CIA World Fact Book – Yes, even the CIA can and should be referred to when you are looking for information to help you close a deal or prove a point and get what you want. The CIA World Factbook provides information on the history, people, government, economy, energy, geography, communications, transportation, military, and transnational issues for 267 world entities. Use the link below to access this powerful source of information.

  https://www.cia.gov/library/publications/the-world-factbook/

- Finance – looking for sources to help you with financial support or facts to support what your points are? Check with these sources – Yahoo! Finance, The Motley Fool, Edgar Online, and Forbes. These are just a few of the reliable financial sources that you can tap into to help you.

- Health Research – Issues concerning health can be found at these popular and trustworthy sources.

  United States National Library of Medicine

  WebMD

  PubMed

- Beenverified.com – Beenverified is a paid research service that provides public records and other research sources and information all in one place. If you can't find information through a free source, this site is a cheap and reliable source you can pay for and get almost anything you need. The site normally offers a free trial for up to 7 days for as little as $1 or so.

You can pay the $1 get all the information you want and then cancel within the 7 days. You will have gotten all the information you need for only $1 dollar, a bargain that can't be beat.

- Truthfinder.com – Truthfinder is also a paid research service that is very similar to Beenverified. Take a look at either of these as an alternative to finding the information you need to support your position.

Rule Two: Don't be afraid to admit that you don't know something. Why are people reluctant to gather information? Because to find things out, you have to admit that you don't know, and most of us are extraordinarily reluctant to admit that we don't know. So the first rule for gathering information is: Don't be over confident. Admit that you don't know something and admit that anything you do know may be wrong.

This can disarm your opponent and take him or her off guard because they have a sense that they have the upper hand. Often you will get the information you need to end the negotiation in your favor.

Rule Three: Don't be afraid to ask questions. There is something to the old adage "ask and you shall receive". You may be pleasantly surprised when you ask a question. Often you will get what you need.

Even if they don't answer the question, you'll still be gathering information. It might put pressure on the other person or annoy them so much that they blurt out something they didn't intend to. Just judging the other person's reaction to the question might tell you a great deal. If you want to learn about another person, nothing will work better than a direct question. Develop boldness about asking questions. You will find that it works more to your advantage than to your disadvantage and you will definitely become a better negotiator.

When you get over your inhibitions about asking people questions, the number of people willing to help you will surprise you.

Rule Four: Ask open-ended questions. Successful negotiators understand the importance of asking direct questions and of taking the time to do it properly. What's the best way to ask? Rudyard Kipling talked about his six honest serving men. He said, "I keep six honest men serving-me." (They taught me all I know); their names are What and Why and When and How and Where and Who. Of Kipling's six honest serving men, I like Why the least. Why can easily be seen as accusatory. "Why did you do that?" implies criticism. "What did you do next?" doesn't imply any criticism.

If you really need to know why, soften it by rephrasing the question using what instead: "You probably had a good reason for doing that. What was it?" Learn to use Kipling's six honest serving men to find out what you need to know.

You'll get even more information if you learn how to ask open-ended questions. Close-ended questions can be answered with a yes or a no or a specific answer. What you want is the person to respond without feeling they are being boxed in. Give them latitude to speak without feeling intimidated or that they are being set up. The results, often times, are you will receive information that will help you move on to the next point in the negotiation process. The information could be the difference between a successful negotiation ending or not.

For example, "How old are you?" is a closed-end question. You'll get a number and that's it. "How do you feel about being your age?" is an open-ended question. It invites more than just a specific answer. "When must the work be finished?" is a closed-ended question. "Tell me about the time limitations on the job," is an open-ended request for information.

Rule Five: Where you ask the question makes a big difference. Power negotiators also know that the location where you do the asking can make a big difference.

Successful negotiation often is similar to the sale of real estate. In real estate the commonly known point about how well a piece of property will sell is where it is located. Location, location, location is the phrase used in the sale of real estate all the time. If a property is located in a favorable and desirable place it will sell much quicker and bring a higher price than a property located in an undesirable location.

Negotiation is no different. The location where a negotiation takes place is an influence, although subtle, that can have a huge impact on the outcome.

If you meet with people at their corporate headquarters, surrounded by their trappings of power and authority and their formality of doing business, it's the least likely place for you to get information.

People in their work environment are always surrounded by invisible chains of protocol-what they feel they should be talking about and what they feel they shouldn't. That applies to an executive in her office, it applies to a salesperson on a sales call, and it applies to a plumber fixing a pipe in your basement.

When people are in their work environments, they're cautious about sharing information. Get them away from their work or familiar environments and information flows much more freely. And it doesn't take much. Often that's all it takes to relax the tensions of the negotiation and get information flowing. And if you meet for lunch at your country club, surrounded by your trappings of power and authority, where they are psychologically obligated to you because you're buying the lunch, then that's even better.

Even meeting for a cup of coffee at Starbucks rather than in formal surroundings makes a difference. Always try to have negotiations in an environment where its neutral and neither party is faced with the challenge of feeling they are meeting on the other person's turf. Every edge in a negotiation counts.

Rule Six: Ask other people. If you go into a negotiation knowing only what the other side has chosen to tell you, you are very vulnerable. Others will tell you things that the other side won't and they will also be able to verify what the other side has told you. Start by asking people who've done business with the other side already or have some knowledge about the other. This may not always be possible but, where it is, don't fail to take advantage of this tactic. If you are diligent in doing this, it will amaze you-even if you thought of them as competition-how much other people are willing to share with you.

Be prepared to horse trade information. (Give information to get information). Don't reveal anything that you don't want them to know. However, the easiest way to get people to open up is to offer information in return. People who have done business with the other side can be especially helpful in revealing the character of the people with whom you'll be negotiating. Can you trust them? Do they bluff a great deal in negotiations or are they straightforward in their dealings? Will they stand behind their verbal agreements or do you need an attorney to read the fine print in the contracts?

Next, ask people further down the corporate ladder than the person with whom you plan to deal. Let's say you're going to be negotiating with someone at the main office of a nationwide retail chain. You might call up one of the branch offices and get an appointment to stop by and see the local manager. Do some preliminary negotiating with that person. He will tell you a lot, even though he can't negotiate the deal, about how the company makes a decision, why one supplier is accepted over another, the specification factors considered, the profit margins expected, the way the company normally pays, and so on.

Be sure that you're "reading between the lines" in that kind of conversation. Without you knowing it, the negotiations may have already begun. For example, the Branch Manager may tell you, "They never work with less than a 40 percent markup," when that may not be the case at all. And never tell the Branch Manager anything you wouldn't say to the people at his head office. Take the precaution of assuming anything you say will get back to them.

Next, take advantage of peer-group sharing. This refers to the fact that people have a natural tendency to share information with their peers. At a cocktail party, you'll find attorneys talking about their cases to other attorneys, when they wouldn't consider it ethical to share that information with anyone outside their industry.

Doctors will talk about their patients to other doctors, but not outside their profession. Power negotiators know how to use this phenomenon because it applies to all occupations, not just in the professions. Engineers, controllers, foremen, and truck drivers; all have allegiances to their occupations, as well as their employers. Put them together with each other and information will flow that you couldn't get any other way.

If you're thinking of buying a used piece of equipment, have your driver or equipment supervisor meet with his counterpart at the seller's company. If you're thinking of buying another company, have your controller take their bookkeeper out to lunch. You can take an engineer from your company with you to visit another company and let your engineer merge with their engineers.

You'll find out that unlike top management-the level at which you may be negotiating-engineers have a common bond that spreads throughout their profession, rather than just a vertical loyalty to the company for which they currently work. So, all kinds of information will pass between these two. Naturally, you have to watch out that your person doesn't give away information that could be damaging to you. So be sure you pick the right person.

Caution them carefully about what you're willing to tell the other side and what you're not willing to tell. Then let them go to it, challenging them to see how much they can find out. Peer-group information gathering is very effective.

Power negotiators always accept complete responsibility for what happens in the negotiations. Poor negotiators blame the other side for the way they conducted themselves.

As a negotiator, you should have the attitude and accept that there's no such thing as a bad negotiation. There are only negotiations in which we don't know enough about the other side. Information gathering is the most important thing we can do to assure that the negotiations go smoothly.

Key Points to Remember

- Never go into any negotiation without having as much knowledge and information as you can about the other side and the points that will be discussed.

- Take time to research and find the data, facts, and figures that back up what you want to say. Use the sources that are in this book and others to support your positions.

- Don't be afraid to admit you don't know something. Often this will loosen the other side up and they will share information that helps move the negotiation process along.

Chapter Four

Use Reluctance to Move Negotiations Forward

Be reluctant when you are seeking to buy, sell or get something you want. Reluctance will help you get additional information you need to close the deal in your favor.

Let's say that you're looking to buy a whole suite of new furniture for you and your staff.

How would you get a salesperson to give you the lowest possible price? One way would be to have a salesperson come to your office and view the entire facility and let them get a good feel for what the potential sale would mean to them. This gives motivation to the salesperson to really want your account, especially if the potential sale is a high dollar value.

You could also let them know that you may look at other furniture providers as well but will hold off until you see what they can do for you. Have them provide you with a presentation and let them go through it entirely all the while acknowledging the good points and suggestions they will likely make.

You ask all of the questions that you could possibly think of and when you finally can't think of any additional questions, you say, "I really appreciate all the time you've taken. You've obviously put a lot of work into this presentation, but unfortunately, it's just not the way we want to go; however, I sure wish you the best of luck."

You pause to examine the crestfallen expression on the salesperson's face. You watch he or she slowly package their presentation materials. Then at the very last moment, just as their hand hits the doorknob on the way out, you come back with this magic expression. There are some magic expressions in negotiating. If you use them at exactly the right moment, the predictability of the other person's response is amazing. Continuing on you say, "You know, I really do appreciate the time you took with me. Just to be fair to you, what is the very lowest price that you can sell the suite of furniture for?"

I think you'll agree with me that more likely than not, the first price the salesperson quoted to you is not the real bottom line. Of course, the salesperson has been trained and also knows from experience not to quote the lowest price first. The first price is what I call the "testing price." It's the number they wish they could get and will test to see if the prospective buyer will take. After all you never know until you ask.

If you said yes to the first price offer, the salesperson would probably run back to their office and make an announcement to everybody saying, "You won't believe what just happen to me" and brag about how it was so easy to get the sale by just quoting a price and telling you they offer an already discounted price from which they don't negotiate and you just accepted it even though you could have gotten a better deal if you had just said no to the first offer.

So, the first price quoted is almost always the testing price. Somewhere within the universe of negotiations there is always a "walk-away" price, a price at which the salesperson will not or cannot sell. You, as the negotiator seeking the best price usually won't know what the walk-away price is. You must do some probing, some seeking of information. You must try some negotiating tactics and techniques to see if you can figure out the salesperson's walk-away price.

When you play Reluctant Buyer, the salesperson is not going to come all the way from the test price to the walk-away price. Here's what will typically happen. When you play Reluctant Buyer, the salesperson will typically give away half of his or her negotiating range. If the furniture salesperson knows the bottom line is $125,000 which is $50,000 below the list price of $175,000 he or she will typically respond to the Reluctant Buyer tactic with, "Okay, here's what I can do for you. This is one of our finest lines of furniture, but we're having a yearend clearance sale on inventory and I have a little flexibility.

If you'll place the order today, I'll give you our absolute best discount and sell the entire furniture suite to you for $150,000." They will give away half their negotiating range, just because you played the Reluctant Buyer role. Remember that when people do this kind of thing to you, it's just a game that they are playing on you. Effective negotiators don't get upset about it. They just learn to play the negotiating game better than the other side.

Reluctance works when you're selling something too.

One thing to remember about the process of negotiation is that you are always selling something. It doesn't matter if it's a product, a service, a concept, or even yourself. One way or the other we as human beings are always selling something. Although many people, if not most, abhor the concept of having to sell something, the reality is nothing happens until a sell is made.

Get into the mindset and train yourself to think in terms of selling as nothing more or less than a persuasion and negotiation process. Sometimes the process opens and closes immediately. Sometimes it takes a process of time – days, weeks, months or sometimes years depending on the mission and goals that are at stake.

Showing reluctance from a selling standpoint can be just as powerful as from a buying standpoint.

Imagine for a moment that you are the owner of several real estate properties. One of them is a condominium that is located in a decent area and you've been renting it out for a period of time. However, there has been a recent local rent control law passed and you will not be able to raise the rents on that property for a very long period of time.

You had planned to raise the rent on the property because the rent you've been receiving is well below the market already. However, because of the new legislation you can't do anything but accept the rental rate that is currently in place.

On the other hand, the Home Owners Association has just increased the monthly HOA fees that you have to pay on that property and there has been a new county tax assessment that added some additional property taxes you now have to pay as well.

Finally, the tenants you have aren't the best and are always creating problems with maintenance costs and fees that cause you to pay in upkeep more than what you are comfortable with.

The mortgage payment on the property is now more than the funds coming in every month to service the debt and maintain the property. In short, you are operating the property at a loss now. You need to get rid of it, especially since lately you've been performing some of the maintenance on the property yourself to save money and no longer able to enjoy the leisurely weekends you've become accustomed to.

It suddenly dawns on you that this scenario isn't going to get any better. In fact, it's likely going to get worse. You decide you are going to sell this turkey as quickly as possible and walk away from it as soon as you can. You also decide you will sell the property as a "for sale by owner" property in order to save on real estate broker fees. You list the property in the classified ads and on other for sale by owner publications.

Almost immediately you get several inquiries on the property and one day while you're working on the property making necessary repairs to help it sell you hear a knock on the door. You answer it and it's an attractive well-dressed couple. They introduce themselves and tell you they are looking to move into the neighborhood as their company has transferred them to the area and they saw your for-sale by owner sign in the yard.

They ask if they can come inside and look at the property. You, of course, invite them in. After they've looked at the property, the female of the couple, with a smile on her face, says she really likes the property and its conveniently closeto work and she especially likes the remodeled area you've just finished in the kitchen and bathroom.

She looks at her husband and say's "honey I really like it. Can we get it"? At this point your heart starts to race in your chest because you know instinctively this is likely going to work for you if the negotiations are handled well. Silently, you thank God for your good fortune.

Nevertheless, you tell them that since you've been putting so much time, energy and money into the property and the new remodeled design, you're seriously thinking about keeping it as one of the properties in your real estate portfolio due to the increase of value that has been added because of the remodeling you've completed.

However, you say to them "I can see how this property would perfectly fit into your situation right now based on what you've told me so, just to be fair to you, what is the very best offer you can make me on the property? You ask this question because the asking price you posted on the for-sale sign and in the classified ads is quite a bit higher than you know you would really accept.

Using this technique – Reluctant Seller – squeezes the negotiating range before the negotiation even starts. If you've done a good job of building the other person's desire to own the property, they will have formed a negotiating range in their mind. Let's say you posted the sale price at $300,000. It is entirely possible that the prospective buyers may be thinking "We'd be willing to go $280,000 but if we could get this property for $250,000 we'd take itimmediately."So their negotiating range is from $250,000-$280,000. Let's say you are willing to sell the property for $275,000 and this price is reasonable for the market in that area for the property you are selling.

Just by playing the Reluctant Seller, you will have moved the couple up through that range. If you had appeared eager to sell, they may have offered you a low ball figure like $225,000 to test the waters. Playing the Reluctant Seller got the opening offer much closer to the final amount you want to sell it for. In fact, given the range you can likely get the full price you truly want ($275,000). After all you have the emotional motivating factor of a wife who has already decided she wants the property. Her husband's motivation more likely will want to be to satisfy her desires.

Remember, people make decisions motivated by emotions and later justify the decision with logic.

Having this basic understanding of human nature will take you far along the road of the negotiating process. Keep in mind that when people pull this kind of technique on you that it's just a game that they are playing. As a negotiator don't get upset about it. They usually just have a bit of negotiation skills themselves.

Key Points to Remember

- Play the Reluctant Buyer when you are buying something. It works to draw out the best possible offers the other side will likely make in your favor.

- Always play the Reluctant Seller. Using this technique is a great way to squeeze the other side's negotiating range before the negotiation even starts. The other person will typically give away half his or her negotiating range just because you use this strategy.

Chapter Five

How to Use Time as a Negotiating Ally.

If you have the information and the power (or perceived power) to make something happen you are in a powerful negotiation position. When you know the time limitations of the other side you are in an even more powerful position. Time limitations, if they are real, will put pressure on the negotiation process and usually speeds up the negotiations as the end of the time period approaches.

The natural tendency of most human beings is to put things off until the last minute then when the last minute comes there is always frantic action to get the thing done before the deadline. Sound familiar? Well, guess what? Negotiations and those negotiating are no different.

Getting things done at the last minute just seems to be the lot of most human beings. Perhaps you're thinking that you are different. Really?

Think about these examples. April 15, every year is the deadline to file income taxes. When do you think most people file their taxes? Usually, at the last minute. The U.S. Postal Service even stays open until midnight to accept last minute filings of income taxes from all over the country. If you have a deadline to get a project done, unless you are different from the norm, you wait until the time is almost up before you get serious about it and then cram everything into getting the project out on time.

Procrastination seems to be a gene most people either are born with or they acquire over a period of time. Either way, deadlines affect when a person, company or government will be more likely than not to be under pressure to make a decision and get something accomplished. The closer the time gets to the deadline the more you can gain concessions in your favor during negotiations.

The key, however, is to know whether the deadline is the true deadline or a gambit to just throw you of and make you think it is the real deadline.

I can personally attest to the fact that 95% of the negotiations that I have successfully reached in my legal career on behalf of hundreds of clients as well as myself almost always came at the last minute – the deadline for the date of trial, just before the jury was ready to announce its verdict or just before the judge said he or she had reached a decision and was ready to announce it.

This was not usually because I personally wanted to wait for the last minute, it was because the other side knew there was a deadline and just would not agree to any conclusion until the last minute or until the deadline was present and it was a gamble for them to wait to see what would happen after the deadline passed.

Knowing these facts (again having the information first) I would always use it to raise the bar higher the closer the time came to the deadline. I would ask for more money on behalf of my client as the time neared the deadline because I knew pressure was mounting on the other side and facing uncertainty they usually wanted to now "just get it over with"

You can use deadlines as a strategy in negotiations as they are very effective. Just remember, they work both ways. Deadlines can be used against you as well, especially by someone who is skilled enough to understand the pressure of deadlines and how they affect human behavior.

Negotiators who recognize that deadlines affect everyone equally can use them to defuse costly stalling tactics. For example, car salespeople sometimes try to draw out price negotiations, hoping the amount of time you've invested will increase your commitment to making the deal. To defuse this strategy, try beginning your negotiation for a new car by informing the salesperson that you have only an hour to make a possible deal.

I've used the above tactic on numerous occasions to successfully bring a negotiation to a close. I simply state up front what my deadline is. It's really quite simple. I might begin the negotiation by informing the other side that I have only a certain amount of time to conclude the negotiations, say in two hours, because I have another very important appointment I must get to.

Many experienced negotiators would say this would be a huge mistake because it gives the other side ammunition to just stall and wait until the two hours are almost up to see if concessions would be made in their favor the closer the time gets to the two-hour deadline I announced.

I think not. Here is why. The reason I announced the two hour deadline was to put pressure up front on sides, mine and theirs.

There is nothing that says I won't walk out and there will be no deal at all if we don't get it done in two hours. I just might do that. If the announcement is done in a sincere and convincing manner there is no reason for the other side to assume this will give them an advantage at all. It also gives me another tactic to use should we get close to reaching a deal and the two hour time limit is just about up. I simply say, "give me a moment I need to make a phone call", call my legal assistant and tell her to rebook my other appointment for a later time.

I may even ask the other side to use one of their phones to do it. This only adds to my power in the negotiations because it makes it appear I am negotiating in good faith and even looks like a concession to the other side. This encourages the other side to make concessions also. (Remember the concept of reciprocity).

Because deadlines put pressure on everyone, they can get talks moving again. Don't be afraid to set deadlines and commit to them.

There are times when it's wise to tell your fellow negotiators about your deadlines. This advice holds true even when you have little power and are desperate to make a deal. A "one-sided" deadline will only put more pressure on you to concede quickly.

In negotiation, you'll have many opportunities to use deadlines strategically. Don't be afraid to set them and to reveal them.

Just remember revealing or not revealing a deadline should be part of your negotiating strategy. Sometimes it's advantageous to reveal your deadline and sometimes it may not be. It will always depend on the circumstances and who is on the other side of the negotiation.

Key Points To Remember

- When negotiators tell their opponents about an existing final deadline, they get better deals. Why? First, because both sides are more likely to work toward an agreement before the deadline passes, you reduce your risk of walking away with nothing.

- Second, when an opponent knows about your deadline, they will make concessions much more quickly.

Chapter Six

Ask and You Shall Receive. Ask for more than You Expect to Get.

Using another example regarding, Henry Kissinger, former Secretary of State, and heralded as one of the best negotiators during his time, he made a practice of asking for more than what he wanted during any negotiation process. Sharing one of his negotiation tactics, he said "Effectiveness at the conference table depends upon overstating one's demands." Just think about that concept for a moment. Most people are reluctant to ask for things because they are either too timid, feel they would be asking for too much, would be taking advantage of the other side or just have a lack of understanding about the power of asking for what you want.

Unfortunately, the culture that most people are raised in, particularly in the western world, creates a fearful environment for asking for things and we get lulled into not asking for things that we should be asking for because we fear the answer is going to be no. That's unfortunate, because a good negotiator not only should ask for more than what is expected to be received but should also embrace and welcome any no responses.

A no does not mean the negotiation is over with. It should be looked upon as another bit of information that you can use to move the negotiation along.

Getting very comfortable with asking and expecting great things to happen should be one of the mindsets that you should develop as you travel the negotiation highway.

Think of some reasons why you should ask for more than what you really expect or why, as Henry Kissinger says, "Overstate your demands."

- Why should you ask the store for a bigger discount than you think you have a chance of getting?

- Why should you ask your boss for an executive suite although you think you'll be lucky to get a private office?

- If you're applying for a job, why should you ask for more money and benefits than you think they'll give you?

- If you're dissatisfied with a meal in a restaurant, why should you ask the manager to cancel the entire bill, even though you think they will take off only the charge for the offending item?

If you're a salesperson:

- Why, if you are convinced that the buyer wants to spread the business around, should you still ask for it all?

- Why should you ask for full list price even if you know it's higher than the buyer is paying now?

- Why should you ask the other person to invest in the top of the line even when you're convinced they're so budget conscious that they'll never spend that much?

- Why should you assume that they'd want to buy your extended service warranty even though you know they've never done that in the past?

If you thought about this, you probably came up with a few good reasons to ask for more than you expect to get. The obvious answer is that it gives you some negotiating room. If you're selling, you can always come down, but you can never go up on price. If you're buying, you can always go up, but you can never come down.

The key to asking for more than what you truly expect to get is you must make sure that your position is always within the realm of reasonableness. Don't ask for something that is so ridiculous that it makes no sense whatever. If you do, your credibility is shot and the negotiations go down from there.

What you shoot for and should be asking for is your MRP – your Maximum Reasonable Position. In other words, what is the most you can ask for and still have the other side see some reasonableness in your position?

Be sure when you use this technique that you have facts, figures, experiences and theories that make your position appear reasonable so that if you are challenged on why you are asking you can be comfortable that what you are asking for is not out of the question.

The less you know about the other side, the higher your initial position should be, for two reasons:

1. You may be off in your assumptions. If you don't know the other person or their needs well, they may be willing to pay more than you think. If they're selling, they may be willing to take far less than you think.

2. If this is a new relationship you will appear much more cooperative if you're able to make larger concessions. The better you know the other person and their needs the more you can modify your position.

Just remember, it works both ways. If the other side doesn't know you their initial demands may be more outrageous.

If you're asking for far more than your maximum reasonable position imply some flexibility. If your initial position seems outrageous to the other person and your attitude is "take it or leave it" you may not even get the negotiations started. The other person's response may simply be "Then we don't have anything to talk about." You can get away with an outrageous opening position if you imply some flexibility.

Let's say you're negotiating to purchase a parcel of real estate. As you enter into negotiations, you might say, "I understand that you're asking $350,000 for the property and based on everything you know that may seem like a fair price to you. So perhaps you know something that I don't know but, based on all the research that I've done, it seems to me that we should be talking something closer to $275,000." Now, the seller's thought may be "That's ridiculous." I'll never sell it for that, but he does seem to be sincere, so what do I have to lose if I spend some time negotiating with him just to see how high I can get him to go?"

If you're a salesperson you might say to the buyer, "We may be able to modify this position once we know your needs more precisely, but based on what we know so far about the quantities you'd be ordering, the order preparation and the delivery schedules, our best price would be $4.95 per unit. At that the prospective buyer may likely be thinking, "That's outrageous, but there does seem to be some flexibility there, so I think I'll invest some time negotiating further to see how low I can get the seller to go."

Unless you're already an experienced negotiator, here's the problem you will have with this. Your real MRP –Maximum Reasonable Position - is probably much higher than you think it is. We all fear being ridiculed by the other person or persons. So, we're all reluctant to take a position that will cause the other person to laugh at us or put us down. Because of this intimidation, you will probably feel like modifying your MRP to the point where you're asking for less than the maximum amount that the other person would think is reasonable.

Another reason for asking for more than you expect to get will be obvious to you if you're a positive thinker: You might just get it. You'll never know unless you ask.

In addition, asking for more than you expect to get increases the perceived value of what you are offering. If you're applying for a job and asking for more money than you expect to get you implant in the personnel director's mind the thought that you are worth that much. If you're selling a car and asking for more than you expect to get it positions the buyer into believing that the car is worth more.

Another advantage of asking for more than you expect to get is that it prevents the negotiation from deadlocking. People are wired to always push back at the first offer in any negotiation. By asking for more than you expect and it looks reasonable, the other side will generally counter the offer with something. If you start out asking for what you've determined is your bottom line to begin you have no negotiation room.

However, if you've boldly asked without even a hint of doubt for something that is much more than what you are willing to settle for what might happen is the counter offer will be much more than what you would have settled for in the first place.

By asking for more than you expect you create an environment where the other side feels that they can win as well. Effective negotiators know the value of asking for more than they expect to get. It's the only way that you can create an environment in which the other side feels they won too.

Key Points To Remember

Ask for more than what you expect to get because:

- You might just get it.
- It gives you some negotiating room.
- It raises the perceived value of what you're offering.
- It prevents the negotiation from deadlocking.
- It creates an environment in which the other side feels they won.

Chapter Seven

Never Accept the First Offer Made. It's not the Real Deal.

One of the fundamental principles of negotiation is the knowledge that you should never accept the first offer made in reaching a solution in negotiations. Why, because it automatically triggers two thoughts in the other person's mind.

Let's say you've wanted a yacht for years and you've been going to boat shows and hanging around the water every chance you get. Your desire is been mounting and one day you realize you have enough money to perhaps get that dream boat if the price is right.

You head down to the local harbor and you browse around the boats and look at all of them with glee and imagine what it would be like to own one of those sleek vessels, be able to cruise along the shore, feel the breeze and enjoy the scenery with the people you care about most. As you walk around the harbor slip you see this magnificent 35foot yacht with a for sale sign on it. You take a look and it has everything you dreamed of and want in a yacht.

It just so happens that the boat owner is onboard and when you inquire about the price you find that the asking price is $40,000. Your reaction is not immediate but you know your boats because you've been searching and gathering information on them for a long time. This model is one of the top yachts in the market and if it is in decent shape $40,000 is a fair price.

You ask about the condition of the boat. The seller produces a recent professional survey of the boat and its condition and allows you to read it. Nothing major is wrong with the boat. It just needs the standard maintenance that is required by all yachts in a harbor.

You decide this is the yacht for you, the one you've been waiting for. The price is within your range and the boat is solid and you want to snap this yacht up before it's taken by someone else. However, you think it would be a mistake to offer the seller the asking price of $40,000, so you decide to make a super low offer just to see what the seller's reaction would be.

You say to the seller "This boat doesn't meet all of the requirements that I've been looking for in a yacht, but I'll give you $32,000 for it."

You're waiting for the owner to react with a "what are you crazy look or response." Instead what actually happens is the seller looks at you momentarily and then says "you've got a deal." Does this response and acceptance by the seller make you jump for joy? Do you immediately feel that you are one of the greatest negotiators around and you just pulled off the steal of the century? I doubt it.

You're probably thinking something like:

1. What's wrong with this boat? Is there something that wasn't shown in the survey?
2. Is the seller hiding something from me that will make this purchase a big mistake on my part?

More likely than not you start to have a sinking bad feeling about this deal. Likely you think "I could have done better," and "something must be wrong."

Human beings are wired to negotiate with one another. We have an expectancy that the other side is always looking for the best result for themselves and that's true in almost all situations. Because of this natural expectancy, people are used to bargaining with one another and reaching a solution only after haggling back and forth. What that does is set up expectations of reality and when that expectation is shattered the natural tendency or emotion is to feel something is wrong.

You had done your research on boats and knew this particular model was one of the best. You knew that the professional survey would have shown if anything major was wrong with the boat. You saw the survey was recent. All signs were go, so when your $32,000 offer was accepted you should have been thinking "Wow, what a terrific deal I just got." "Couldn't have gotten a lower price." That's what you should be thinking but very likely you would not be thinking that.

Rather, you would most likely think "I could have done better." You see, it doesn't have anything to do with the price it has to do only with the way the other person reacts to the proposal. How the person reacted caused you to have a perception that it was too easy. It created doubt about your ability to gage the value of the boat and a host of other emotions likely are stirring within you at the moment, none of which make you feel very good.

In fact, one of your main thoughts would be "Something must be wrong." So, your mind immediately starts to make calculations and decisions like "I want to make a further inspect on the boat and check more into the survey before I finalize the purchase." "Something must be going on that I don't understand if the seller is willing to accept an offer that I didn't think would be accepted." "Maybe the market for this yacht model has changed and my research didn't catch that."

These are the kinds of thoughts and reactions that will occur in anybody's mind if the response is yes to the first offer.

This is a very easy negotiating principle to understand, but it's very hard to remember when you're in the thick of a negotiation. You may have formed a mental picture of how you expect the other side to respond and that's a dangerous thing to do. Never assume.

Here's the point I want to make. Don't fall into the trap of saying yes too quickly. The reason is because it automatically triggers in the other person's mind:

1. I could have done better.

2. Something must be wrong. Turning down the first offer may be tough to do, particularly if you've been calling on the person for months and just as you're about to give up, she comes through with a proposal. It will tempt you to grab what you can. When this happens, be a Power Negotiator-remember not to say Yes too quickly.

Key Points To Remember

- Never say yes to the first offer or counter-offer from the other side. It automatically triggers two thoughts: I could have done better and something must be wrong.

- The big danger is when you have formed a mental picture of how the other person will respond to your proposal and she comes back much higher than you expected.

Chapter Eight

Watch out for these Two Negotiation Traps.

It's not fair and the silent treatment. Neither of them is good for you.

In a negotiation you are not there to be fair. Your goal is to get what you want or need. Anything less is really unfair to you, if you want to talk about fairness.

Most people are taught a concept, as they grow up, that "one should be fair." Generally, that means people should conduct themselves in a manner that negotiations or making decisions that affect situations where their two sides differ the opposite sides should strive to agree on things that provide both sides the things that they want or as near to what they want as possible.

That's great in theory, but the reality is we live in a world where often it is dog eat dog, so to speak, and the opposition is there to take as much as they can for themselves. Yet, in negotiations, the cry is always "let's be fair," or one side complains to the other that what is being proposed is not fair.

When you are negotiating anything, no matter what it is, keep in mind your goal is to get what you want or need out of the negotiation process. It is not to be fair from a conceptual standpoint. Here's the challenge in any negotiation. What may be fair in your mind may be entirely different than what fairness is to the other side. It's in the eye of the beholder.

Getting what you want or need out of a negotiation is fair. It is up to the other side to achieve the same goal for themselves or for whomever they represent.

One of the philosophies of negotiations I have learned over the years and most definitely keep in mind when I'm negotiating on behalf of myself or representing someone else is a slogan from Dr. Chester L. Karras, a world renowned negotiator and coach. He coined the phrase, "In business as in life – you don't get what you deserve, you get what you negotiate."

My negotiation skills and the things that I've negotiated in life changed when I read this and contemplated it and then started to put it into action. It's true. Business and life is nothing but a series of negotiations. It's not about what one might deserve. Besides, who is to make the choice of what you deserve better than you?

No matter what, you will encounter situations where there is a claim that what you propose is "not fair." It's going to happen. How you respond and handle it is the key to successfully concluding the negotiation.

Being fair is understanding as much as possible about the other side and knowing what they want to accomplish out of the negotiation. After all, if they get what they want or as close as possible to what they want and they agree, then it's fair. This is why you want to do research and understand and know as much about the other side as possible before you start negotiations.

Find out the other party's agenda and embrace it. It is very important to understand the point of view of the other side. Find out before negotiations begin, if you can, what represents successful results for the other side. How can you help make them look better? Put yourself in their shoes. This is the process of putting yourself into position to get what you want by helping them get what they want.

If you can do it without compromising and destroying the chance of getting what you want or need out of the negotiation process, then that's the route you should take. In the process of doing this you prevent the other side from feeling that "this is not fair."

Avoid the "Let's split the difference negotiation tactic."

Sooner or later, if you are involved in negotiations at all, you will get to a point in trying to reach a good conclusion, particularly where money is the issue, to "split the difference." This is just another way of saying "let's be fair." I have faced this issue and question numerous times during negotiations on behalf of clients in settlement conferences and mediations. Even judges have weighed in during settlement conferences suggesting that the opposite sides should split the difference.

The major problem with this tactic is that its usually designed to convince each side to give a little to get some of what they want. The theory behind this process is the claim that if each party leaves the negotiation feeling that neither of them won totally against the other then usually it's a good settlement or negotiation result. In other words, if both sides leave a little unhappy then neither side took advantage of the other and both sides left with some of what they came to get.

This is a very common negotiation tactic. As a power negotiator you should reject this type of approach. Your job is to negotiate to get what you want or what the person or entity you are representing wants. While you must always conduct yourself in a professional and ethical manner, being "fair" is not a Holy Grail standard that should be followed. Remember, "fair' is in the eye of the beholder.

What is fair to one may not be fair to the other. The job of a good negotiator is to keep the eye on the prize and do what is necessary to reach the ultimate goal of getting what you want from the negotiation process.

Negotiations are not a search-and-destroy mission.

The one sure thing that I know about business is, if you have your foot on someone else's neck, at some point in the future, that person will have his foot on your neck. The goal in negotiations should be to get as close to a win-win conclusion as possible but include all or most of what you or the person or entity you are representing want to achieve.

If your side of the winning is going to be big do not clean the table and just leave. Take your winnings and give the appearance and action that you want the other side to earn and win their way back. Make it a positive loss and an earned opportunity ahead. Always see the future. You never want to treat any one negotiation as the last opportunity for a win-win result. You need to look at the whole picture and at the whole relationship (especially at your long-term interests) as opposed to obsessing over the current situation. Even when you win, you cannot afford to lose that perspective.

Silence is not always golden in negotiations. Say what you mean and mean what you say.

There is a place and time to just shut up during a negotiation. Silence is one of the most powerful tactics to use in successful negotiations. However, it must be used at the appropriate time. It should never be used in a manner to not say something – being silent about it- because you feel the other side will take something offensively or take advantage of the situation.

Negotiation involves the gathering of information along the way. If there is a need to say something don't be silent about it. Determine the best way to say it or introduce the concept into the negotiation. Unless the other side knows the important points that you require to be addressed and dealt with your chances of getting what you want out of the negotiation are lessen.

How to use silence in your favor

People who are really powerful are also very often the quietest. When it comes to communication between human beings, silence can be incredibly uncomfortable. We are hot wired to talk and interact with one another and when this stops, especially during a negotiation, it is unsettling and our instinct is to try and fill that void and ease the tension, often without thinking. In those situations, the first one to speak usually loses. The other side gets nervous and proceeds to talk and give up information that usually can be used against them.

Because of this natural instinct, silence can be a power tool, and if you really want to get the best results during a negotiation, you need to make sure you're using silence correctly.

Words are the tool of every negotiation. Without words, there can be no effective negotiation on either side. It's about what is said, how it is said, and what is really meant when it is said. The more the other side talks the more information acquired which can be used to help understand their position and how to shape a response to best meet their needs. However, if a period of silence shows up, both sides have a strong tendency to feel or go into a panic mode.

What generally happens is both sides feel tension and want to fill in the gap. Perhaps the minds even think that there is now an impasse and the parties cannot reach a conclusion. Fear of loss sets in and both sides will start to talk all at once just to fill in the gap. The tendency is to get back to normal where everybody was talking.

During negotiation people just don't like silence. Inwardly it drives them crazy. It's just natural and this provides you with the power point.

Using silence effectively and powerfully requires one to have the ability to know when to shut up.

One of the most important times for you to use silence as a negotiation tool is right after you present your position to the other side. Make your point and just shut up. It should be like crickets (quite). Resist the tendency to fill in the silence. Be quite and study the reaction of the other side. The tension to break the silence is on the other side. If you break the silence it is usually with talk that doesn't add anything positive to getting what you want and more often than not will be a position that takes away from the negotiating position you've just put forth. This is the last thing you want to do.

The opposite of being silent immediately after you've put forth your position at the negotiation table is when the other side has made a proposal to you. There is no advantage to you if you respond quickly and start to talk without taking time to process the proposal and let it sink in. Give yourself some time to think. You need to be silent to do this. If you start talking while you are considering what the proposal is you might miss an important part of the opposite sides proposal. Be silent and measure what you want to say.

Using silence as a negotiation tool is one of the most powerful tactics in getting what you want. In fact, silence is not something that comes up often in most negotiations and when it does usually we don't know what to do about it. Generally, we just want to fill in the gap and start talking when we should be listening and looking for a sign from the other side that will signal what our next move should be.

Lastly, it should be understood that silence can also be interpreted by either side that the negotiations have stalled and there is nothing else that can be accomplished. If this circumstance should occur, it is not recommended that silence end in the negotiation parties leaving the discussion table. You always want to provide some closure to the conversation. So, if you've hit a wall where it no longer seems productive to keep talking, it may be wise to agree to take a break from the negotiation efforts and reconvene at another time.

This leaves the door open for each side to reflect on where they are and what the next best moves should be. It also allows each side to think about the time, effort, and expense that has already been expended and which will be lost if silence caused them to discontinue negotiations.

Often, once each side has reviewed the status of where they are, they come to the realization that they are not that far apart and have agreed on more points than they disagree and should come back to the negotiation table with renewed intent to negotiate in good faith and create a viable conclusion for both sides.

Key Points To Remember

- Avoid the negotiation trap of "let's split the difference".

- Use silence as your power partner. Determine when to just shut up. Don't panic and fill in the silence gap. The first one to talk during the silence gap usually loses.

- Beware of the complaint "its not fair." Remember, in negotiations you don't get what's fair. You get what you negotiate.

Chapter Nine

What to do With the "I Don't Have Authority" Negotiation Response.

One of the most frustrating situations you can run into is trying to negotiate with someone who claims they don't have the authority to make a final decision. Often this may be a ploy and simply a negotiation tactic that's being used on you. It is usually used to delay and stall for time to reflect, gain more information, and more importantly to set up in your mind that whatever proposal you've made may or may not be acceptable.

Unless you realize that this is simply a negotiating tactic that's being used on you, you may have the feeling that you'll never get to talk to the real decision-maker.

During my litigation career, I sat across the table on numerous occasions with parties, attorney's and clients, that often claimed they did not have the authority to accept a proposal and needed time to call or check with the person or persons in authority before they could respond. Sometimes, it was a true statement, but in most instances it was a stalling tactic and one designed to gain advantage.

To be honest, I've used the same tactic on numerous occasions when representing clients in negotiations. When engaged in settlement negotiations, I often would ask for the highest amount of monetary settlement that would not seem totally ridiculous with the knowledge that permission from my client to accept less would not be a problem. The client had already given me a figure or, in most cases, complete authority to accept whatever figure that made good economic sense on their behalf.

Under these circumstances my tactic was always to get the other side to offer as near to or above the target amount. I would then say, you've been fair and it doesn't look like we are too far apart, but I need to review this with my client and I'll get back to you tomorrow with an answer."

The next day I would get back to them and say, "Wow, my client still wants to see if this matter can be resolved and I thought he/she might be favorable to your proposal, but they just won't go along with the current offer." I may even give them some reasonable basis for the client's position for leverage purposes. Then I would say, I am authorized to accept some sum of money that is more than what they had previously offered. Often times this would work, and I would get more money than what I was authorized to settle the case for in the first place. Remember, in negotiations you don't get unless you ask.

Even if you are not an experienced negotiator and you don't negotiate on behalf of others on a regular basis, you will be faced with this negotiation tactic along the road of your life. If you've ever purchased a car or been with someone who has you've encountered this negotiation technique.

You walk onto a car dealer's lot and after some strolling around you find the car of your dreams. It has everything you want in it. The color is perfect, and you decide you want this car now. There is a salesperson who talks to you about the car and you are ready to buy the car, assuming you can get a break on the price. Here's what the salesperson does, he takes you into a room asks you some questions and fills out some forms.

You tell him what price you want to pay (that's your offer). What does the salesperson say? Something like this. "You know, I think I can get this deal for you at the price you are offering but I need to speak with my manager first." (Higher authority).

The salesperson leaves and comes back with the manager who promptly greets you with a big wide smile and a hearty handshake. She tells you that the price you are offering is a bit low for this model and all the luxurious options that it has. However, for another $1000 they can do it for you. What do you do? Of course you can walk away and not take the deal, but now you are emotionally involved. You want that car. After all it's only an additional $1000.

You have just been subjected to the higher authority tactic. This happens thousands of times a day throughout the car buying process across the country.

Now that you have this book and know how to negotiate you can smile confidently when this occurs, whether at the auto dealership or anywhere else you meet this technique, and use some of the following tactics.

When faced with the "I don't have final authority" negotiation tactic here's what you can do.

To be effective and smooth, your first approach should be to try to remove the other person's resort to higher authority before the negotiations even start. This is done by getting them to admit that they could make the decision if the proposal was irresistible.

Here's an approach you can use. Simply ask the question of the other side in the negotiation. "Let me be sure I understand, if we come to a meeting of the minds is there any reason why you wouldn't make a decision today?" It's exactly the same thing that the car dealer will do to you when, before he lets you take the car for a test drive, he says, "Let me be sure I understand, if you like this car as much as I know you're going to like it, is there any reason why you wouldn't make a decision today?"

Because they know that if they don't remove the resort to higher authority up front, then there's a danger that under the pressure of asking for a decision, the other person will invent a higher authority as a delaying tactic. Such as, "Look, I'd love to give you a decision today, but I can't because my spouse has to look at the car or Uncle

Roy is helping us with the down payment and we need to talk to him first."

One of the most frustrating things that you may encounter is the taking your proposal to the other person and having them say to you, "Well, that's fine. Thanks for bringing me the proposal. I'll talk to our committee (or our attorney or the owners) about it and if it interests us we'll get back to you." Where do you go from there?

If you're smart enough to counter the higher authority tactic before you start, you can remove yourself from that dangerous situation. So before you present your proposal to the other person, before you even get it out of your briefcase, you should casually say, "Let me be sure I understand. If this proposal meets all of your needs (That's as broad as any statement can be, isn't it?), is there any reason why you wouldn't give me a decision today?"

It's a harmless thing for the other person to agree to because the other person is thinking, "If it meets all of my needs? No problem, there's loads of wriggle room there." However, look at what you've accomplished if you can get them to respond with, "Well, sure if it meets all of our needs, I'll give you an okay right now."

Look at what you've accomplished:

You've eliminated their right to tell you that they want to think it over. If they later say they need to check with a higher authority, you say, "Well, let me go over it one more time. There must be something I didn't cover clearly enough because you did indicate to me earlier that you were willing to make a decision today."

You've eliminated their right to refer it to a higher authority. You've eliminated their right to say, "I want our legal department to see it, or the purchasing committee to take a look at it."

What if you're not able to remove their resort to a higher authority? Let's say you begin with "If this proposal meets all of your needs is there any reason why you wouldn't give me a decision today?" And the other person replies, "I'm sorry, but on a project of this size, everything has to get approved by our projects committee. I'll have to refer it to them for a final decision."

Here are the three steps that Power Negotiators take when they're not able to remove the other side's resort to higher authority:

Step number one-appeal to their ego. With a smile on your face you say, "But they always follow your recommendations, don't they?" With some personality styles that's enough of an appeal to ego, that they'll say, "Well, I guess you're right. If I like it, then you can count on it." But often they'll still say, "Yes, they usually follow my recommendations, but I can't give you a decision until I've taken it to the committee."

If you realize that you're dealing with egotistical people, try preempting their resort to higher authority early in your presentation, by saying, "Do you think that if you took this to your supervisor, she'd approve it?" Often an ego-driven person will make the mistake of proudly telling you that he doesn't have to get any body's approval.

The second step is to get their commitment that they'll take it to the committee with a positive recommendation. So you say, "But you will recommend it to them-won't you?" There are only two things that can happen at this point. Either she'll say, yes, she will recommend it to them, or she'll say, no she won't-because . . . Either way you've won. Hopefully, you'll get a response similar to, "Yes, it looks good to me, I'll go to bat for you with them."

But if that doesn't happen and instead they tell you that they won't recommend it you're still ahead, because any time you can draw out an objection you should say "Hallelujah" because objections are buying signals. For example, nobody will object to your price unless buying from you interests them. If buying from you doesn't interest them, they don't care how high you price your product or service.

Let me prove this to you. Give me the opposite of the word love. If you said hate, think again. As long as they're throwing plates at you, you have something there you can work with. It's indifference that's the opposite of love. Think about that for a moment.

When they're saying to you, like Rhett Butler in Gone With the Wind, "Quite frankly, my dear, I don't give a damn." -that's when you know the movie is about over. Indifference is your problem, not objections.

Objections are buying signals. So when you say to them, "You will recommend it to them, won't you?" they can either say, yes they will, or no they won't. Either way you've won. Then you can move to step three:

Step Three: The qualified "subject to" close. The "subject to" close is the same one that your life insurance agent uses on you when he or she says, "Quite frankly, I don't know if we can get this much insurance on someone of your age. It would be "subject to" you passing the physical anyway, so why don't we just write up the paper work "subject to" you passing the physical?"

The life insurance agent knows that if you can breath enough to fog a mirror during that physical, he or she can get you that insurance. But it doesn't sound as though you're making as important a decision as you really are. The qualified "subject to" close in this instance would be: "Let's just write up the paper work 'subject to' the right of your project committee to reject the proposal within a 24-hour period for any specifications reason." Or, "Let's just write up the paper work 'subject to' the right of your legal department to reject the proposal within a 24-hour period for any legal reason."

Notice that you're not saying subject to their acceptance. You're saying subject to their right to decline it for a specific reason. If they were going to refer it to an attorney it would be a legal reason. If they were going to refer it to their CPA, it would be a tax reason and so on. But try to get it nailed down to a specific reason.

So the three steps to take if you're not able to get the other person to waive his or her resort to higher authority are:

Appeal to the other person's ego.

Get the other person's commitment that he'll recommend it to the higher authority.

Use the qualified subject-to close.

Key Points To Remember

- Attempt to get the other person to admit that he could approve your proposal if it meets all of his needs. If that fails, go through the three counter tactics

  1. Appeal to his ego

  2. Get his commitment that he'll recommend it to his higher authority

  3. Go to a qualified subject-to close

- If they are forcing you to make a decision before you're ready to do so, offer to decide but let them know that the answer will be no, unless they give you time to check with your people.

- If they're using escalating authority on you, revert to your

---

Being able to use and handle the resort to higher authority is critical to you when you'repower negotiating. Always maintain your own resort to higher authority. Always try to remove the other person's resort to a higher authority.

Chapter Ten

You'll Have to Do Better Than That! the Magical Phrase that Gets Amazing Results.

One should always keep in mind during any negotiation process that it's a process. Some negotiations take longer than others. Some may take a few hours or less, some can extend to days, weeks, months or even years when national and international stakes are involved.

Keeping in mind that negotiation is a process allowingyou to have a mindset to go with the flow and see what happens. Having this kind of mindset allows flexibility to use a tactic or phrase that is often referred to as the vise grip technique. Of course, a vise grip is a tool that is used to apply pressure points to an object once the tool is attached. If the grip is too loose at first to hold the object in place, more pressure is applied until there is such a firm hold that the job can be finished.

In negotiations the vise grip technique is applied similarly. Let's say you are a small company that provides widgets that your prospective customer uses to produce its final product. You or your sales force make a great presentation to the prospect who seems to be genuinely interested in what you have to offer. Although, the prospect has been doing business with one of your competitors your company makes a compelling enough presentation to peak the prospect's interest.

Finally, the prospect says "I don't want to make any promises, but I would be willing to seriously consider switching from my current vendor if you can sell me your widgets for $2.95 each over the next year."

You respond with the magic phrase "I'm sorry you'll have to do better than that." Notice the object is now $2.95 per widget. By using the vise grip phrase you've now put the object inside the grip and starting applying pressure points to bring the price to a more favorable place that you want it to be.

> Of course, you or your sales team have already done your homework and have the information before you entered the sales negotiation about the price of the widgets within the industry, competitors' price range, and etc.

Here's the point. Once you respond with "I'm sorry you'll have to do better than that", an experienced buyer (or negotiator) would come back with "Tell me just how betterthan that do I have to do?" The object, of course, is to pin you down and use the vise grip to tighten you down to a price that is acceptable to the buying company.

However, it is a good chance you may not be dealing with an individual that has good negotiation skills. In that case they will almost always give up big concessions in their negotiation range simply because you use that phrase. Remember, it doesn't hurt to ask. After all you are just negotiating.

For this technique to be most effective there is one thing you should always do immediately after you say, "You'll have to do better than that." You must be quiet. Be silent. Remember the power of silence we talked about in the prior chapter? Don't say another word. The pressure is building on the other person on the other side. It may be they will come back with a price that is much better than you anticipated. You could be defeating your purpose if you say anything beyond the vise grip phrase.

It is possible that the prospect or negotiator on the other side has some negotiation experience. Once you stop talking they may ask how much better they need to be or they could just be silent like you. What then? Do you sit there and stare at each other and make it a battle of silence? Remember, the general rule is the first one who breaks the silence generally will lose because it usually means the person speaking is making a concession of some sort.

However, think of this tactic. If the person on the other side is playing the game of silence, you could simply repeat what you just said before. "You'll have to do better than that." Yes, you were the first to speak but you made no concession. Quite the contrary, what you did was put more pressure on the other side now to respond. They may say "I heard you the first time" or something else. The point is the silence has been broken and now you are in control to move the negotiation along.

If may be that they come back with a price that is different but still not to your acceptance. You could then use the higher authority tactic. Simply, state you need to get back to your board of directors, the sales committee or whatever makes it appear reasonable. This keeps the negotiation open and gives you opportunity to go and think about a better approachand come back with a different offering of sorts.

Another story about former Secretary of State Henry Kissinger and how he used the vise grip phrase to get the maximum excellence out of people who worked for him.

The story took place during the Vietnam War. Secretary Kissinger asked an undersecretary of state to prepare a report on the political situation in South East Asia. The undersecretary worked very hard on getting the report just right. He conducted extensive research, checked and rechecked facts and presented his findings to Mr. Kissinger. For the undersecretary'ssurprise, the report was very quickly returned to him with a note written across the report that said, "You'll have to do better than this. H.K."

The undersecretary went back and found more information, added graphs and charts and etc. and presented the revised report to Mr.

Kissinger. The undersecretary was confident that the report would be acceptable and was in fact one of his best pieces of work. However, again it came back to him with the notation, "You'll have to do better than this. H.K." Now the undersecretary was flabbergasted and frustrated. He called upon his staff to assist him and worked tirelessly to get more information exhausting every possible area or source that could possibly provide any relevant information.

When the report was finally completed for a third time he had significant reservations about submitting the report and made a request to meet with Mr. Kissinger in person to present the report. During the presentation of the report he said "Mr. Kissinger, you've sent this back to me twice. My entire staff has dedicated the last two weeks to this report. Please don't send it back again. It's not going to get any better than this. This is the best I can do." At this point Mr. Kissinger simply placed the report on his desk and said, "In that case I will read it."

This technique works no matter if you're bargaining with a street vendor, person to person in a personal situation, negotiating a huge contract, representing a large national or international organization or nation to nation.

It's just a matter of having enough courage to use it and once you do. Just be silentand see what happens. The advantage may be even more than you expected.

Key Points To Remember

- To gain a better negotiation result whenever the other side makes an offer you don't want to accept respond with "You'll have to do better than that.

- If the other side also remains silent for a period of time repeat "You'll have to do better than that."

- If the other side responds to you with a proposal you need time to think about or gain more information use the "higher authority tactic"

Chapter Eleven

In Negotiations You Get By Giving, But Don't Give Until You Create A Return From the Other Side.

The negotiation process should be a give and get environment. Without it there is little likelihood that a successful conclusion will occur for either side.

Anytime the other side asks you for a concession in the negotiations you should automatically ask for something in return. You should do this for two main reasons. First, you want to appear reasonable and send a message that you have some flexibility and are willing to engage in the negotiation process to get to a conclusion. Second, you want to ensure that the negotiation process will move forward. Without making some concessions along the way the negotiation process will be subject to stall and nothing gets accomplished.

Although you should give to get, what you give is the important thing. Never give anything that will be so substantial that you lose your bargaining power in the negotiation. Give small things that are significant enough to show the other side you are serious and want to make a deal but never are the deal breaker until you get into a position to get what you want.

Do tradeoffs. This technique works to get small concessions along the way in order to set up the final conclusion where you get to where you ultimately want to be.

For example, let's say you owned a condo that you just sold, and the buyers ask you if they could move some of their belongings in to the condo 10 days before the closing of escrow. Although, you are reluctant and would never allow them to take full possession of the property until the closing is complete and the payment has cleared, you see an advantage in allowing the storage of some things before the final closing.

This technique will get them even more involved in the feeling that the deal is done and get them emotionally attached and far less likely to create any problems in completing the deal. You are anxious to get rid of this condo because you no longer use it much and it has become a financial noose around your neck making the monthly payments on something that you aren't getting any return on any longer.

This makes you eager to make a concession, but you should remember this rule: No matter how small the concession they're asking you for, always ask for something in return. You might say to them, "Let me check with my wife (or someone else) and see how they feel about that, but let me ask you this: If I do that for you, what will you do for me?"

I have used this technique often in negotiations on behalf of my clients during my several decades of law practice. Give a little to get a bit more and continue to move forward to the ultimate goal. In one of my cases, I represented a client in a wheelchair who had been denied accommodation in a hotel that he booked a room in. The room did not have grab bars nor did it have an accommodating shower that my client could use for his toilet purposes. Before, filing a lawsuit, the hotel was even given notice of its violations under the Americans with Disabilities Act (ADA). Nevertheless, no accommodations were provided. After filing the lawsuit, the attorney for the hotel wanted to resolve the matter and we entered into negotiations.

It became very clear to the hotel's attorney that liability on his client's part was very clear and if the case went to trial his client would lose and be subject to substantial monetary damages, payment of my attorney fees as provided under the law, and for costs that my client had already incurred in bringing the lawsuit.

During the settlement negotiations, the hotel owners wanted to settle,but the amount of money damages my client demanded they pay they said they couldn't afford. This was a sticking point for my client. The hotel ownership asked if there was a figure less than what was on the table. I deflected the question and simply asked "if there was a lower settlement number my client would possibly consider, what else could you offer that might make him change his mind?" I already knew the hotel had to bring the hotel into compliance with statutory law, so I knew that could not be an option for further negotiation.

What they came back with was an offer, in addition to some money, to provide my client with a number of times he could come to the hotel and stay for free after the compliance issues were taken care. This was a nice hotel that carried a national name brand. It just so happened that my client often had relatives that came to visit him as well and the rooms could be offered to them for free.

I discussed this with my client and he was delighted with the idea. His staunch stand on the original money amount changed and we were able to get the deal done. The hotel was delighted because they had to come up with less actual cash and the rooms would help them save money because oftentimes the hotel had vacancies that were not making any money anyway. The number of times for the use of the rooms and their actual market value increased the value of the settlement even more than what the original settlement demand was in the first place.

The point is this all occurred by giving something but getting something in return. So the moral of this story is, during negotiations, when you are asked to give something be open and ready to give, but always ask for something in return. You might just get something that is even more valuable than what you expected.

In addition, by asking for something in return, you elevate the value of the concession. When you're negotiating and give something away that you don't have to, always make a big deal out of it. You may need that later.

Let's go back to the sale of the condo for a moment. You've sold the condo and you've allowed them to move a few things in. The day before the close of escrow and your receipt of the check there is a final walk through for final approval and sign off as was agreed between you and the buyers. The buyers notice that an overhead light switch does not work and the overhead fan in the guest room does not function.

Under those circumstances you're able to say, "Do you know how it inconvenienced me to let you put all your stuff in here so you wouldn't have to pay the last several days of your storage costs elsewhere? I did that for you, and now I want you to overlook these small problems.

Using this technique cuts away the grinding process. It creates an atmosphere of give and take on both sides and allows for a solution that makes both sides feel they've accomplished what they came for. This is the key reason you should always use the tradeoff technique. If they know that every time they ask you for something, you're going to ask for something in return, then it stops them constantly coming back for more.

In order for this technique to be most effective you must use it in proper form. Don't become confrontational with the technique by using terms phrases like "If I do that for you, you will have to do this for me", this makes the negotiation atmosphere too confrontational. Becoming confrontational at a very sensitive point in the negotiations – when the other side is under pressure and is asking you for a favor can wreck the entire process.

Instead keep it simple and just always say "If I can do that for you what can you do for me." Of course, if you're representing more than yourself you would use terms like us or we.

When using this technique "If I do that for you what can you do for me," you must be prepared for the response to be something like "We can't do anything for you, "or something like you "You get to keep us in the negotiation and us not walking away." Don't be upset at this, because you had everything to gain by asking and you haven't lost anything.

In fact, you've now gained more valuable information that can help you continue to negotiate. They've made a commitment. At this point you can revert to a position of insisting on a tradeoff by saying something like, "The people I represent likely won't agree to that unless you're prepared to give something of value in return," or unless you're willing to provide a different amount of money than we've been talking about.

The one theme that should always run through every negotiation is this. You must always ask for what you want. If you don't ask, you don't get.

Key Points To Remember

- When asked for a small concession by the other side, always ask for something in return.

- Use this expression: "If I can do that for you, what can you do for me?

- You may just get something in return or it elevates the value of the concession so that you can use it as a tradeoff later.

- Most important it stops the grinding process.

- Don't change the wording. Use, "If I can do that for you, what can you do for me? Anything else might come off as too confrontational.

Chapter Twelve

Use the Flinch or Wince Technique (Shock and Awe Negotiating)

The flinch or wince technique is one of the oldest negotiating tactics in the realm of negotiation. Used at the right moment it changes the dynamics of negotiation and can almost always be used to gain some traction in your favor.

Here's something to always keep top of mind in negotiations. When people make a proposal or offer to you, they are looking for your reaction. They may not even think for a moment that you'll go along with their request. Usually, it's just thrown out to see what your reaction will be.

Don't forget the reality that people make decisions based on emotions and back those decisions up later with logic. When people are negotiating their emotions are shown by the way they act more often than by what they say. We learn and gage where a person might be coming from by what we see. How they physically respond to what is being said or done is key to successful negotiations.

Knowing that visual cues are important you can use them to your advantage. The flinch wince technique is a very powerful negotiation tactic. The reason is because the other side can immediately see your reaction to what has been said or done and how you react sends a strong message. We are influenced more by what we see than any of the other 5 senses human beings react to.

Fact: Approximately 65 percent of the population are visual learners: Mind Tools

Fact: The brain processes visual information 60,000 times faster than text: 3M Corporation 2001.

Fact: 90 percent of information that comes to the brain is visual:Hyerlve, 2000

Fact: People can remember the content of 2500 pictures with over 90 percent accuracy 72 hours after looking at them for only 10 seconds. A year later participants had 63 percent recall of those same images. Crockett, 2010;

I provide the above facts about visual effect to emphasize the importance of the flinch negotiation tactic. While the flinch is one of the oldest negotiation tactics, it is one of the least used. A flinch is a visible reaction to an offer, price or proposal during a face-to-face negotiation. The objective of the tactic is to make the other side uncomfortable about the offer they just made. The ultimate strategy is to gain the upper hand and negotiate a better deal.

An example of how the flinch or wince tactic works is the scenario of say a software supplier making an offer to a business owner that needs a complete customer relations system which would be a substantial outlay of money on the part of the business owner. The software supplier outlines all the features and benefits of the system and the buyer is very interested and then comes the price.

Immediately, when the price of the system is provided, the business owner physically reacts with a frown and pursed lips and exclaims" You want how much? There's no way." The business owner appears shocked and surprised that the software supplier could be bold enough to state such a figure.

Here's the kicker. Unless the software supplier is skilled in negotiations, the most likely response will be one of two ways.

(1) The supplier will become very uncomfortable and begin to try to rationalize the price or;

(2) They will offer an immediate concession

Either way the use of the flinch has changed the dynamics of the negotiation. If the supplier tries to rationalize the price he makes his software a commodity that can be shopped against all other software suppliers offering the same or similar product. This puts the supplier in a price war against competitors and under pressure to lessen the price to close the sale.

Arguing price against another competitor is never a good position to be in. It makes the price the most important point and that's almost always a losing proposition from a seller's standpoint. It makes the service or product a simple commodity that lessens the value of the other benefits and features.

Of course, if the software system supplier's response is the second option, then the flinch has done its job as well. Either way it's a powerful tactic if done with skill.

People use the flinch or wince negotiation tactic all the time. Kids, who are master negotiators by the way, use it all the time. When a child wants something, a flinch could turn into a tantrum, sulking, crying or any number of things. They want candy or ice cream in a crowded store with people all around. When told no, the child starts with a pained expression that escalates into a little dance of irritation, maybe even falling on the floor.

People are watching all around and guess what? The child often gets what he or she wants at that moment. They don't think about the consequences later. They are in the moment and they pull the flinch. It works.

Now you may be saying, "Roy that's great for a child but I'm an adult. I am not going to act like a child in negotiations." Of course, you won't, if you are a professional. As adults in a professional setting it's not befitting to act like a child. But we can flinch, and as a negotiation tactic it's a wonderful tool. All you need to know is how to use it, deliver it, and how to deflect it when used on you.

It's simple. When a proposal or offer is made to you that you don't like or don't want to entertain, you flinch as if you just got shocked with a jolt of electricity. Here's what will likely happen. The person who made the offer or proposal will usually want to empathize with you. He or she may quickly relent or try to ease your pain. It's just human nature to want to relieve pain unless the other side is a skilled negotiator or just a person who has no empathy. People will do just about anything to avoid pain, even empathetic pain.

The flinch can be whatever physical or verbal signs you use and may depend on the situation surrounding the negotiation. Nevertheless, the flinch works. Try it out.

I've used the flinch tactic on numerous occasions as a lawyer negotiating on behalf of clients. A perfect example of the use of the flinch tactic occurred during the taking of a deposition of one of my clients. Before the deposition my client and I had talked about the value of his case and quite frankly had come to the conclusion that it was not the strongest case on a factual basis. Nevertheless, our strategy was to be bold and argue the law and how it could be applied in the most positive manner for the client.

We had agreed my client would not give in to any low balled offers, if made during the deposition. Sure enough during the deposition, the opposition's attorney slide a check across the table in front of my client made out in the sum of $40,000 and with a sly smile asked him if he would settle for that sum right now because his client was prepared to fight all the way otherwise.

My client looked at me and his face became flush red and he looked very irritated. He then turned and with a scowl on his face he asked the opposing attorney "is that offer the amount you want to pay my lawyer for his attorney's fees? It must be because I won't be settling this case for near that amount." The opposing lawyer took the check back and asked to take a short break. My client had just pulled off a fabulous flinch, red faced, upset and with a forceful voice.

After the break, the opposing lawyer resumed the deposition. Once again, during the deposition, he paused and this time he shoved another check across the table to my client in the amount of $60,000 and asked if he would settle the case for that amount right now. My client flinched again. He started twitching and moving around and said he was ready to leave right then because he had no interest in settling his claim for such a ridiculous amount. I suggested we take another break to allow my client to calm down so we could complete the deposition.

During this break a different attorney who also represented the opposing side approached my client and me and said "I told him before the deposition that those tactics he just pulled would likely not work and would only infuriate your client. Tell me what your client wants and let's see if we can get this case settled today." Ultimately, we settled the case for $145,000 that very day which was well over the sum of $100,000 my client was willing to settle for in the first place.

What happened was my client used the flinch even though he had no idea what it was. It was just his natural reaction to the situation. That's what made it so powerful. It immediately caused the other side to reassess their position and to have empathy. In fact it generated empathy from the co-counsel of the other side so much that he actually argued on our behalf. Needless to say, my client was very happy with the results and so was I. That experience also crystalized the flinch negotiation tactic in my head. It has served me well over the years in different negotiation situations.

Using the flinch should come as natural as possible. If you feel uncomfortable with a proposition or offer, you just need to verbally and physically communicate that to the person delivering the offer via a flinch.

Be mindful of the fact that the flinch can also be used on you. When it is you should react accordingly. Either the person flinching is really pained by your offer, or they are faking to be. Either way it indicates you have some work to do. It is a signal that you need to change up and move forward with a different proposal.

The key to responding to the "flinch" is to recognize that it is an opportunity to express your position more fully. Instead of lowering your expectations it can serve as a springboard to exchange viewpoints and build a stronger relationship. The best way to handle the flinch is to tell your story as though the other person had said, "Please tell me more." Don't let it bother you or cause you to lose confidence in your position. Use it as an opportunity to explore win-win possibilities.

The flinch is most effective in person to person negotiations because you can communicate visually and verbally to send the most powerful impact. It can also be done on the phone through voice inflection. If you try it through writing or a text, the power is diminished because it is difficult to communicate flinches in writing and maintain the proper tone.

Like any other skill, it takes practice to effectively pull off a flinch. However, it is well worth the effort because whether you realize it or not you are negotiating every day so try some flinching on some of your next transactions. The flea market, buying a car, even at retail outlets are good places to practice. Also, watch for others using the tactic on you.

Key Points To Remember

- Flinch in reaction to a proposal or offer from the other side. They may not expect to get what they're asking for, but if you don't show surprise you're communicating that it's a possibility.

- A concession often follows a flinch. If you don't flinch, it makes the other person a tougher negotiator.

- Assume that the other person is visual unless you have something else on which to go.

- Even if you're not face to face with the other person you should still grasp in shock and awe. Telephone flinches can be very effect also.

Chapter Thirteen

Body Language – the Truth Teller In Negotiations.

Closely related to the flinch negotiating tactic is the use of body language in negotiations. The flinch tactic is almost exclusively communicated through body language. That's one of the reasons it's so effective.

You must be mindful of your body language before and during negotiations. Skilled negotiators watch counterparts and negotiation opponents before entry into negotiation as well as during negotiations. Observation of body language before negotiations is called baselining. A baseline is the observing of how a person reacts when they are not engaged in negotiations and how they are communicating non-verbally under those circumstances such as casual talk.

The body languages used during such situations are unconscious and done naturally. Observing and gathering this information can help tremendously in reading the person during negotiation. If you can observe the person before starting negotiations it can help you create a baseline to see how the person communicates non-verbally. This can help you during negotiations. This may not be possible all of the time but should be part of your process in preparing for a negotiation.

If you aren't in control of your body language, it doesn't matter how much you've prepared for a negotiation. Your body language will either help you or it will hinder you during negotiations. Body language is one of the things about human beings that never lie and if you become skilled in reading it you will be a very powerful and effective negotiator whether for your own personal use or on behalf of others in a professional capacity.

First impressions are extremely important in negotiations particularly if it's the first time your opponent has seen or met you. How you walk, stand, gesture, look, nod or use your eyes can all be summed up in a matter of moments to determine how the opposite side will perceive you and make a mental note of how the negotiations may go.

Remember the chapter about the power of perception? Your body language, in part, plays a big role in how you will be perceived as well as how you will perceive the opposition.

The study of body language is called Kinesics which is all about non-verbal communication.

Here's the good news about Kinesics or body language. You already know it. It's just been running on autopilot without you even noticing it.

Think about it, how many times have you noticed or picked up on the body language of a person and quickly assessed the situation and the message that was being sent and it turned out to be right. Likely you remember it has happened countless times before.

Expressions and body language surround us every day. We learn through natural experience what most of the body language means and yes some of it is universal, so it applies across cultures, creeds, nations and etc. A smile is universal. Handshakes and how they are applied are universal. Frowns of disapproval are usually universal. I could go on with more, but you got the picture.

Now just think about it for a moment. You've been reading people's body language and doing it on a daily basis and interpreting it and coming to your conclusions of what the messages are. Many of the conclusions you reach are correct. You then make a quick decision on how you will react to the message you've just been sent and taken action or speak vocally accordingly. You don't even think about it, it just happens. That's because we've been taught to read body language and react to it on autopilot. Many of the skills to read body language are already in us.

Becoming a skilled negotiator and knowing how to use body language to maximum benefit is just bringing to mind the skills we already have and also learning others and then creating a systemic way of consciously being mindful of body language when we negotiate so we can use it to our advantage.

While there are many studies, schools and disciplines on the vast types and meanings of body language and how they should be used to advantage there are some that are universally employed in negotiations based upon their past use and effectiveness.

Some of them will jump out at you as you read them and recognize how often you've used them without even thinking – again on autopilot – during the course of your life and in everyday situations. Learn these and consciously apply them in your negotiation efforts in the future. They will help make you a power negotiator.

Beware of first impressions – Let's face it. You and I are guilty of having made snap judgments about people the moment we meet them. How they are dressed, how they look, how they walk, etc. First impressions throughout life are crucial. Sometimes you don't get a second chance.

Research has shown that non-verbal cues have over four times more impact than anything said. According to a study by Davitt, Corporate Social Psychologists:

- First impressions are formed within 7 to 17 seconds of meeting someone.

- 93% of a person's first impression about another person is based upon non-verbal or body language

- 55% of a first impression is what you wear, how you act and how you walk through the door.

- 38% of a person's first impression is determined by tone of voice

- How you shake someone's hand leaves a lasting impression. Give a firm handshake. It should not be a weak handshake ever.

- Only 7% of your first impression is the words you say.

Given these statistics, it is extremely important that you be concerned about the first impressions you make whenever you enter into negotiation with anyone you've not met before. Creating the best first impression sets the tone for how the negotiation will likely go and whether it will be as successful as you would like.

The one thing you never want to do is try to be something that you are not. You must always be yourself and be true to your core but you must temper it with intelligence. The moment you try to be something or someone you're not it will come through loud and clear through non-verbal communication and can destroy any chance you have for a successful negotiation.

Beware with whom you are negotiating and where. Cultural differences can make a big difference in how you should present yourself. Therefore, if you are negotiating with someone from a different culture you should make sure you study and understand how their views are before you meet them. This way you can create the best first impression possible. Some cultures don't shake hands for example and to extend your hand out to shake their hand at the first meeting could be an unintended offense.

Mirroring: The concept of mirroring in negotiations is when one person adopts another person's body language, vocal tone, and behavior, which builds rapport. For example, if the opposite side is engaged, he or she may lean forward and follow your movements. If that's not the case and the person is leaning far back and crossing his or her arms, be sure to find a way to bring the person back in and ask what isn't right. The whole point about mirroring is that you subtly do the same thing with your body as the other person is doing with theirs. This builds rapport and provides an atmosphere within which a successful negotiation conclusion can be reached.

Just remember, if the other person's body languageis sending clear signals that are negative and likely unfavorable to help the negotiation process you don't want to mimic those body expressions. Instead concentrate on finding out why they are tuning you out and do what you can to get them back on track. The success of mirroring depends on mirroring the right people, at the right time, for the right reasons.

According to a study done by Duke University, subtle forms of mimicry can prove useful when you're trying to win someone over. It's known as the "chameleon effect" becausein the same way that a chameleon changes the color of its skin to match the environment people can change behaviors and mannerisms to mirror the person who they're interacting with.

Sometimes the intelligent thing to do is simply not imitate. The key to this technique is you must not be obvious with your mirroring. It must be done in as smooth a manner as possible without alerting the other side that you are doing the same thing that they are doing.

Eye Contact: Out of all of the body language factors that can affect the success of a negotiation, eye contact is one of the most important and faltering eye contact is the most detrimental. There is a saying that "the eyes are the windows to the soul." This is especially true when it comes to effective communication and of course, effective communication is crucial to successful negotiation.

Eye contact should never become a stare. It should be more than a few seconds at a time and should be gaged to make sure the other side knows you are sincere and engaged in the conversation. Polite, but direct eye contact sends a message that "I am here, engaged, serious and ready to make a deal." Weak eye contact communicates lack of engagement, the suspicion that you may be hiding something, or the fact that what you are saying cannot be trusted.

When you are making a point eye contact is very important and should be maintained during the delivery of your point but avert after a few seconds so that it does not become a staring contest.

Nod Your Head to Show Engagement: Showing engagement during negotiation sends a message that you are paying attention and provides a non-verbal cue to the other side that what they are saying is important to you. Remember it's not about you, it's about them. The more you make the person you're negotiating with feel important and that you care and are concerned about helping them get what they want, the more the concept of reciprocity works.

They naturally begin to feel they should give something back to you. That's the corner stone of every negotiation. You must give if you want to get.

Patience: Patience works wonders in negotiations. It is a virtue that you must learn and use in order for your negotiations to be as effective as possible. Often, there is a strong tendency to want to get to the point and quickly close out a negotiation. This is a mistake to avoid.

With patience you can learn more about what the other side needs to make the negotiation work. Patience also creates an environment of empathy which is what you want to show whenever tensions start to increase or the negotiations appear to be derailing.

One way to put patience into practice during a negotiation is to pretend you are talking to a young child or an elderly person or even a grandparent. In those circumstances you need to focus because the child or grandparent might speak softly, and you certainly need to be patient explaining things because topics that are obvious to you may be foreign to them. Don't just assume that the point you want to make is something the other side should already know. Make sure to smile a lot too when exercising patience. This smooths the pathway to negotiation success.

Avoid shaking your leg – I can't tell you the number of times I've been involved in negotiations and I notice that the person or some person on the other side is shaking his leg. Interestingly, I have never noticed this phenomenon in a female. It's always a male for some reason. That isn't to say that females don't engage in this distracting and telltale body language, it's just that I've never observed it during my more than 30 year career.

Bouncing your foot or knee up and down can be a habit – or it can be a sign of nervousness. Either way it should be avoided in negotiating. Shaking your legs while sitting, sends a signal to everyone around you that you are irritated or having a bout of anxiety.

If you're doing it out of habit and you really aren't feeling irritated or having an anxiety attack, to your opponent at the negotiation table it still appears that way. Your legs are the largest part of your body. When they move others notice it.

If you are prone to shake your legs out of habit or are in fact feeling irritated or nervous during a negotiation cross your legs at the ankles. This will stop leg shaking immediately and give you a sense of control and if you are indeed nervous or anxious it will greatly settle your feelings and help you amp up your poise.

Address people at a 45-degree angle or greater

Body position is important when communicating with other people. When you face people straight on, you create a feeling of deep, unconscious confrontation — for both of you. This can be troublesome if you want an easy negotiation. You want to seem as non-confrontational as possible. One of the easiest ways to do this is to adjust your body to a 45-degree angle when addressing others. Just open your shoulders up slightly to them — it doesn't matter if you're standing or sitting. When in meetings, set up the room so that you're not staring at each other across the table. Stagger the chairs. Use your chair's swivel feature. Notice how this eases the situation. You can feel it!

The space between two people is usually described as "body space" or "comfort zone." For negotiation purposes one should be aware of these zones as they can have tremendous affect and effect on how the negotiation process goes.

Standing or sitting too close can give the feeling that one's space is being invaded which makes them feel uncomfortable and pressured. This is something to be avoided. Standing or sitting too far can send the message that you aren't really engaged and not open to serious negotiation.

Body space can also depend on who you are negotiating with and what culture they grew up and live in. Asians generally have a closer body space when talking and discussing business. The distance between can be as close as 1.5 -2 feet. For Americans being this close in a negotiation would be invading space and likely prompt one or both to step back because they feel their personal space is being invaded.

In general, the comfort zone for Americans engaged in serious conversations like negotiations are more in the range of 3-4 feet apart.

Edward T. Hall, author of *The Silent Language,* introduced the science of *proxemics* to demonstrate how man's use of space can affect personal and business relations, cross-cultural interactions, architecture, city planning, and urban renewal. He identifies four different zones that generally apply to Americans when communicating with each other.

1. **Public Zone** – The public zone is generally over 12 feet. That is, when we are walking around town, we will try to keep at least 12 feet between us and other people. For example, we will leave that space between us and the people walking in front.

Of course, there are many times when we cannot do this. What the theory of social distance tells us is that we will start to notice other people who are within this radius. The closer they get, the more we become aware and ready ourselves for appropriate action.

When we are distant from another person, we feel a degree of safety from them. A person at a distance cannot attack us suddenly. If they do seem to threaten, we will have time to dodge, run or prepare for battle.

2. **Social Zone** – The social zone or space is between 4-13 feet. Within this zone, we start to feel a connection with other people. When they are closer, then we can talk with them without having to shout, but still keep them at a safe distance.

This is a comfortable distance for people who are standing in a group but maybe not talking directly with one another. People sitting in chairs or gathered in a room will tend to like this distance.

3. **Personal Zone** – this zone is between 1.5 – 4 feet of space between persons. In this zone, the conversation gets more direct, and this is a good distance for two people who are talking in earnest about something.

4. **Intimate Zone** – This space zone is 1.5 feet or less apart from the other person. It's very close and within arm's reach to allow touch in intimate ways. We can also see more detail of their body language and look them in the eye. When they are closer, they also blot out other people so all we can see is them and vice versa. Romance of all kinds happens in this space.

Entering the intimate zone of somebody else can be very threatening. This is sometimes done as a deliberate play to give a non-verbal signal that they are powerful enough to invade your territory at will.

Be aware that the rules about social distance vary with different groups of people. You can detect this by watching people's reactions. If you feel safe and they seem not to feel safe, back off. If they invade your space, decide whether to invade back or act otherwise.

Turning sideways is an easy alternative for this, as a person to the side is less threatening than a person at the same distance in front of you.

People who live in towns spend more time close to one another and so their social distance may compact somewhat. In a large and crowded city, the distances will be less than in a small town. People who normally live a long way from others will expand their social distances and may even have to lean over towards another person to shake hands and then back off to a safe distance.

People from different countries and cultures also have different rules about social distances. The overcrowded nature of some Asian countries means that they are accustomed to talking to others from a very close distance. Watch a Japanese person talking to a person from a Western country like America. The Japanese will step in and the Westerner will usually step back.

Match their pace of speech. Many people tend to think quickly. You've got lots of details on your mind and want to get on to the next thing. This means you probably speak quickly too. But, understand that the person or persons you're interacting with may not be as speedy as you (especially if they are under stress). If you unload rapid-fire details onto someone who processes information more slowly than you, you'll lose them.

Listen to the speed of their speech and aim to match it. You may need to slow down a bit to meet them where they are. This technique works great over the phone when others can't see you. It can be frustrating at first, but it's well worth the effort.

Leave Your Neck Alone

The neck is a vulnerable area of the body and consistently scratching the back of it or putting your hand near your Adam's apple signals that you're uncomfortable—and possibly even lying. Thanks to his years of experience as an FBI and counterintelligence agent, Joe Navarro, author of "What Every Body Is Saying," discovered that neck touching is one of "the most significant and frequent" behaviors we use when responding to stress.

According to Navarro "This area is rich with nerve endings that, when stroked, reduce blood pressure, lower the heart rate and calm the individual down." "Neck behaviors are extremely accurate, and communicate effectively across all cultures, because they are limbically derived and respond to the world in real time."

> The limbic system is the portion of the brain that deals with three key functions: emotions, memories and arousal (or stimulation)

Although, reading body language and applying it to negotiations is important and useful, when employed, it should be remembered the tactics and techniques described in this chapter are not exact science.

Effective use of body language is an art and a science. While much of what is outlined in this chapter can and should be applied during your negotiation journey keep in mind that they are not absolutes. They are guidelines based upon the study and experience of professionals, scientists, psychologists, and thousands of negotiations practiced by hundreds of successful negotiators including myself. Use them to help you become a power negotiator.

Key Points To Remember

- Always be aware of your body language when negotiating with others. Be aware of theirs too. It can make a huge difference in the success of your negotiating efforts.

- Concentrate on making a very favorable first impression on the people you're negotiating with. First impressions are often lasting impressions so create the best impression first.

- Keep a favorable distance from persons when negotiating with them. Don't invade their comfort zone.

Chapter Fourteen

What Not to Do In Negotiations. Don't Set Yourself Up for Failure

Negotiation is a challenging process. Do it right and you'll seal a deal for a client or complete a favorable negotiation for yourself. Do it wrong and it could be the kiss of death.

No matter how good a negotiator you are things just go wrong sometimes and a deal falls through or never gets to conclusion.

So, how do you act when negotiations break down, or when something careless just slips out?

To help your journey along the negotiation roadhere are some tips on what NOT to say while negotiating.

1. Beware of the word "Between" and how it may be used.

The word between sets you up for making a concession that you may not want to make. It creates a range between one thing or another or from one price to another.

Let's say you're negotiating a deal and price or costs have become the sticking point. The other side wants to know what price you or your client will sell the product or item for or what amount of money would settle the issue if you're negotiating for a settlement of money. You say something like "The item has a cost between $15,000-$25,000."

Which figure do you think the other side will jump on and negotiate around? You guessed it $15,000. You've just set the bar for negotiations on the other side's part. Their goal then becomes to negotiation for less than $15,000 and no more than $15,000.

An experienced negotiator will certainly see this position as advantageous to him or her and zero in on the cheaper price.

Don't fall into this trap of using ranges and ballpark figures. It's better to give the other side a number and stick with it if you can't get them to make an offer first.

2. "I think we're close."

I wish I had five bucks for the number of times during a negotiation the term "I think we're close" has come up. That would be a tidy sum of money.During numerous settlement talks, and especially mediations, the term would be thrown out by the mediator or perhaps the other side "I think we're close." Then the expectation would be for me or my client to agree with that term. In effect adopting it and saying "I think we're close."

If you say those words or agree with the statement when proposed to you, it more often than not sends a message to the other side that you are willing to accept less than what you or your client truly want. You would rather reach an agreement than not.

If the other side has some skill in negotiations they may likely use this instance as an opportunity to go into another direction like stalling and holding out for additional concessions.

Stay away from sending an "I think we're close" message. Work to create an environment where the other side is just as eager to complete a deal as you are.

3. You're asked to throw out a number

I was taught early in my negotiation career that the first side to voice a number or figure during negotiations usually is placed in a position of disadvantage. However, over the years I came to understand that isn't necessarily true.

Because this negotiation theory is so well known (that you shouldn't be the one that throws out the first number) if a number is thrown out by either side it's usually very high or very low depending on the side you are negotiation for. In fact, oftentimes the numbers are so high or so low it hinders the negotiation process rather than helps because the figures used are seen by the receiving side as unrealistic and sets a tone of distrust and sometimes hostility, neither of which is conducive to reaching a favorable results for either side.

If you've done your homework and are prepared when you come to the negotiation table, throwing out the first number can be a good tactic because it is more realistic and can foster the likelihood that a good negotiation result occurs.

Under such circumstances the first number stated in the negotiation can have the effect of anchoring the conversation. In addition, if the opposite side has come well prepared they will also know that the number you threw out is not unrealistic at all. It sends a message that you are savvy and serious about getting results and at the same time sends a message that you intend to get what you came for.

4. Expletives.

Foul language, loud and boisterous talk unfortunately is used sometimes by an opponent during negotiations. This can sometimes happen because the negotiations have become heated and someone just blows up or it could be a designed tactic to gain advantage over you. Either way it pays to be calm.

Never engage back and forth with expletives or other negative reactions. If an absurdly low counter-offer or an annoying stalling tactic has upset the negotiation process take the higher road as best you can in a calm yet forceful manner. Don't take the bait to strike back.

Suggest that a break be taken so participants can calm down. An even better way to respond is to put a label on the emotion that the other person is exhibiting. Remember we humans are very emotional and one of the best ways to deal with emotions is to put a label on it and try to continue the exchange in a way that you get even more information in your favor.

When faced with an emotion you could say something like "It seems like something is irritating you and making you upset" How can I help resolve it?" By making the statement and asking the question, you've immediately shown empathy to the other side and sent a message that you understand something is going on that is bothering him or her. You've now put yourself in a position where they are literally forced to respond in a different manner.

More often than not, they will calm down and give you information that will help you conclude the negotiations in your favor. Chris Voss, a former FBI top hostage negotiator and author of the negotiating book, Never Split The Difference, teaches that labeling is one of the most powerful negotiating tactics to use in such situations. I wholeheartedly agree. Mr. Voss states in his book that labels are powerful and potentially transformative to the state of any conversation.

He goes on to state, "By digging beneath what seems like a mountain of quibbles, details, and logistics, labels help to uncover and identify the primary emotion driving almost all of your counter-part's behavior, the emotion that, once acknowledged, seems to miraculously solve everything else." Since learning of this particular tactic, I've used it on numerous occasions and I can provide testimony that it does work.

Key Points To Remember

- Beware of giving ranges of figures when negotiating by saying something like "a figure between x and x would be acceptable".

- Never agree that "we're close" in negotiations. It sends a signal that you may be willing to make concessions which may not be in your favor.

- Don't be afraid to throw out the first number. It can often help to anchor the negotiations and move it forward rather than work against you.

- Stay calm and use empathy and labeling when faced with expletives and rude behavior during negotiations.

Chapter Fifteen

Avoiding Negotiation Sleaze and Squeeze – Unethical Actions by the Other Side and How to Deal with them.

There will always be situations during negotiations where games are played and ethics go out the window. Some people negotiate with only one goal in mind – to win at all cost, no matter what. That means they will lie, cheat, distort and do all sorts of things that hopefully you would never do.

To be effective at negotiation you must remember to concentrate on the issues and think of negotiation as a game. Understand that the other side is going to try and get the best possible deal from you or the person or company that you are representing as possible.

You must be skilled enough to instantly recognize underhanded techniques and tactics that will be attempted and smoothly counter them.

Armed with knowledge of some of the common tricks used to stealthily extract concessions from you, you will be able to sail the seas of such storms.

Remember, don't get upset when faced with these tactics, just beware of them and deal with them in a calm and forceful manner. Some of the sordid tactics are:

The Decoy

Watch out for the decoy tactic during negotiations. The decoy is designed to get your attention placed somewhere else that might be made to appear to be one of the most important points for the other side so that you will be willing to make a concession on the point that they really are concerned about. It is used to take your attention from what is the real issue.

The best way to deal with the decoy tactic is to stay focused on what the core issues are for you to accomplish in the negotiation. Anything else will distract you and make you less effective on accomplishing that.

Several years ago, I was involved as one of the representatives of a billion-dollar company which was conducting a huge convention in Las Vegas, Nevada. I had made reservations at the hotel several weeks in advance for my wife and me and for a staffer and her daughter. I had wanted rooms very close so we could communicate and have access while we stayed for the activities and programs. In reality, I really wanted adjoining rooms.

When the time came for the convention, we arrived at the hotel and when checking in I was told there was no rooms close to each other available and in fact there were no rooms on the same floor. I was upset, but calm and knew that exhibiting being upset would not help the situation.

Instead, I showed them the reservations that had been made weeks before and that rooms had specifically been set up for us to be close with my staffer and her daughter. Nothing was available I was told.

I asked to speak with a manager. When the manager came, I looked at the manager squarely in the eye and informed the manager that I was one of the representatives for the billion-dollar organization and reminded the manager that thousands of dollars was being brought to the hotel and I would be needing to make a report on how the conventioneers attending had been treated during the convention.

I said I know that hotels often can make accommodations so that people are taken care of as a matter of good business practice. The manager had no idea whether I was a top executive of the company or what position I meant when I said I was a representative. The perception I had given him, however, was that I was important and possibly could have an impact on future business for the hotel.

In addition, what I really wanted was adjoining rooms for me, my wife and my staffer and her daughter.

The manager said "give me a moment sir." Shortly thereafter he came back and said we don't have anything to accommodate your request for adjoining rooms the only thing we have is a suite that has two bedrooms and a living room which is reserved as one of the luxury suites which normally costs several hundred dollars a night.

I looked at him and said, my expectation was to have rooms as requested and for which the company has already paid for – the subtle reminder again that I would likely be making a huge complaint to an organization that could decide not to rebook this hotel again.

What happened next was more than I even expected to get. The manager said "Sir I am going to give you the luxury suite for the same amount of money you would have been charged the rooms. Will that be acceptable?" I said "of course." The suite turned out to be on one of the top floors with bedrooms on both sides and a living room and bar in the middle. My wife, the staffer and her daughter were enormously happy and the convention was a success.

The decoy I used was I was a representative of a huge organization, which I was, but I was not at the executive level. The perception the management apparently had was they would rather give up a suite than have an important representative of the company unhappy. My ultimate goal was to just get rooms on the same floor and perhaps adjoining rooms. My point is the decoy worked.

Cherry Picking

Cherry Picking is a tactic that a buyer can use against a seller with devastating effect, unless the seller is a skilled negotiator and knows his or her options. For instance, if you're thinking of buying a new delivery vehicle for your company, you can use this tactic to your advantage. First, shop around and accumulate information before you make a final decision. Call up delivery vehicle dealers or companies and have all their sales representative make a proposal to you addressing the requirements you have for the vehicle. You'll find that one has a good point in anarea, perhaps a longer-term mile warranty covering major components of the vehicle. Another has more flexible payments and lower interest and another includes free maintenance for an initial period of time.

So, from all these interviews, you piece together the ideal delivery vehicle. Then you go back to the one you like best and say, "I'd like to buy your delivery vehicle except I want to get the longer mile warranty or I want to get the more flexible payments and lower interest." In this way, you create the type of deal and the kind of contract that you want. So, buyers should push for itemized contracts whereas sellers should avoid it.

This tactic is less likely to be used in negotiations where there is already an established history of during business together because it fosters the likelihood that good business relations will be damaged between the parties. Nevertheless, you should be aware of this tactic and be prepared to deal with it under any circumstance. If you're the seller or representing the seller the cherry-picking tactic can be dealt with by building a personal relationship with the buyer.

Another way to handle people who might want to cherry pick you is to build a "roadblock" type presentation and be ready for any cherry-picking ploy. Let's say that you're a landscaping contractor who is trying to sell a landscaping job to a homeowner, and you know she's going to talk to several other better-known landscapers in town. How do you "roadblock" it? The answer is to know more about your competition than the homeowner will ever learn.

So the homeowner says, "I want to check with some other people before I make my final decision." You respond, "I absolutely agree with you." Always agree up front, right? Salespeople should always agree with any objection however ridiculous it is and then work to turn it around. "I absolutely agree with you. You should check with other companies before you make a decision. But look, let me save you some time. Have you talked to Ed Ramos over at Evergreen Landscaping Company? He is one of the well-known landscapers in the area. He uses ABC materials that have this feature, this feature, and this feature; but they don't have this (showing the homeowner specifics and what they do for the landscape).

Then if you talk to Home Depot, Lowes, or the landscape supplier company down at the mall I know most of them personally. The sales people who will talk to you will tell you about the type of trees best planted in this type of yard, the mulch to use and etc., all of which I've put into my presentation to you at the best price you'll find."

By the time you've gone through letting her know how much you know about the competition, she's going to think, "Why on Earth do I need to waste my time talking to all these other people, when this person knows more than I'll ever learn."

To defend yourself against cherry-picking always consider the alternatives of the other side before making a concession. The fewer alternatives the other side has, the more power you have. I refer to this as the "roadblock negotiation defense tactic." If you as a seller refuse to budge on your price, then you force the buyer to pay more from another supplier or use multiple suppliers.

In the case of the landscape job, this would mean that the homeowner would have to bypass you as the main contractor providing all of the services and instead contract with each sub-contractor separately. This may require more knowledge or expertise than the other side possesses or may create extra work and pressure that it is not worth the savings.

The Deliberate Mistake

The deliberate mistake tactic is, in my opinion, an unethical ploy. However, in negotiations just remember, you don't get what is fair, you get what you negotiate. Some people (negotiators) will have no scruples and their goal is simply to win for their side no matter what. You can decide to be that way as well or you can decide to be ethical and have a clear conscious about yourself and on behalf of the persons or entities you represent.

Your own ethics will be called into question in order for this tactic to even work. For example, the seller of products you or your client wants to purchase prepares a proposal and deliberately leaves out or underprices an important item. You see it and know that the negotiations included the omitted item or included a higher price than is listed in the written purchase order.

If you, as the buyer or buyer's representative start to think you can close the deal and get one over on the seller, you become eager to close the deal before the mistake is spotted. What do you do? If you stay silent and hope to pull one over on the seller you're just as unethical as the seller. In addition, if you go down that road, you've set yourself up for the seller coming back and "discovering" the mistake before the deal is concluded and then asking you to pay the extra amount which may be more than you or the client had budgeted for. But, because you have so much time and effort invested in the negotiation at this point you accept the extra anyway.

The better response for you as the buyer would have been to simply point out the issue that the item is not included in the purchase order or is listed at a lower price than quoted by the seller. Don't try to pull one over on the other side. Being unethical is like a disease. If you start it with one deal it tends to spread and becomes a part of your negotiating tool kit. Don't do it. The better solution in this example would be to stay high minded and simply say something like "I assume that you're not charging me for the item you've left out but, that I specifically told you I want. If the price is lower on the purchase order than what was agreed to you could say "I assume that you're charging a lesser price on the item because you're expecting us to continue to do business in the future."

In negotiations, as in life, your reputation is extremely important. Take the high road even if it means you have to walk away from a negotiation occasionally.

Planted Information

There is something about human beings that causes us to have a strong tendency to believe information that we get surreptitiously-something that is not necessarily true but mysterious and prompts us to give it more weight than it should have and influences our decision making. In the real world it is often referred to as "gossip."

Most people just like to hear "gossip" for some reason. Oftentimes, it's not true, but we give credibility to it anyway. The information is planted, and often we believe it. Why? Because we always tend to believe information that we have obtained surreptitiously.

Planted information can be an astoundingly powerful influencer. As an example, let's say a salesman is making an impressive presentation to a panel of buyers whose job is to decide whether a very large contract will be awarded to one of three bidders, one of which the salesman represents.

The salesman really puts everything he has into the presentation using PowerPoint, white board illustrations, and audio affects for emphasis. He is fervently making a plea that they go with his company because it offers the best value in the marketplace. He believes that no competitor can undercut his prices and feels confident that he can close the sale at his asking price of $1,500,000 - until he sees one of the buyers pass a note to another buyer who nods and lays the note on the table in front of him.

Curiosity gets the better of the salesman. He has to see what's on that note. His mind is racing and, as human nature would have it, he thinks negatively instead of positive about what the note might be saying.

This automatically sets a mindset of making concessions without him even realizing it.

He finishes his presentation then approaches the table and dramatically leans toward them. "Gentlemen, do you have any questions?" Out of the corner of his eye, he can now see the note. Even reading upside down, he can see that it says, "Sounds good but a bit high. A bid like $1,375,000 would be better."Global's offer is less. Let's go with them." The lead buyer says, "I do have one question. Your price seems high. We're obligated to go with the lowest price that meets our specifications. Is $1,500,000 the best you can do?" Within minutes, the salesman lowers his price by $125,000. Was the note real or was it "planted information?"

Although, it was just an unsubstantiated note scrawled on a piece of paper, the salesperson believed it because he obtained the information surreptitiously. Even if they had planted it, could the salesperson cry foul later? No, because they didn't actual tell him that the competition's bid was $1,375,000. He obtained the information surreptitiously. He made an assumption that he must live with.

Simply knowing about planted information will help you to diffuse this underhand tactic. Any time that you are negotiating only based on information that the other side has chosen to tell you, you are extremely vulnerable to manipulation. When the other side may have planted the information for you to discover, you should be even more vigilant.

In circumstances like this, the best defense is to always be prepared with information about your competition and be able to address anything that comes up that could make another proposal more favorable than yours. Also understand and be alert for tactics and techniques like planted information that may or may not be real.

Never let greed be the motivating factor inmaking decisions. If the deal is not getting you or your client what you need your alternative plan should always be to just walk away. There will always be other deals or opportunities that provide you with what you need.

Key Points To Remember

- In life you don't get what's fair you get what you negotiate.

- Be prepared for underhanded tactics and techniques during any negotiation. It will happen. The best defense is to always have the best information you can get before the negotiation, so you know more than the other side.

- Be prepared to walk away if it appears underhanded tactics are being used to manipulate you.

Chapter Sixteen

Biblical Principles for Negotiation Success.

One of the best ways to negotiate successfully is to emulate or follow the techniques of great negotiators. There has never been nor will there ever be a better negotiator than Jesus Christ. Humble at the right moment, forceful when necessary, and always gracious toward the other side.

In fact, he often won his negotiations by using logic and allowing the other side to answer their own questions. Once, when the local religious leaders brought a woman caught in the act of adultery to Jesus to test him about the local custom and law that required such a woman to be stoned to death, Jesus did not meet the accusers head on by trying to show them how wrong or unjust their actions were.

This would have given the religious leaders ammunition to attack Jesus for going against the prevailing law. Jesus had announced that he came to fulfill the law and not destroy it. Since Jesus stood for mercy and forgiveness, it would appear he was in a no-win situation. It looked like only thing he could do, since the woman was caught in the act of adultery, was to agree with the law and allow the woman to be stoned to death as required by law. This would have defeated the entire purpose for which Jesus came into existence – to provide forgiveness and bring peace.

Jesus' response was to simply bend down and write something in the dirt (no one knows what he wrote). He then very humbly made a statement to the accusers. "Let he who is without sin cast the first stone". No one made a move to cast a stone against the woman. Jesus then said to her that she was free to go, but don't sin again.

What was Jesus' negotiation tactic? Get the other side to look at itself in terms of what they are really asking. The more you can cause the opposite side to question its own position the better and stronger your position will become.

As I referred to in Chapter Eleven of this book, several years ago, there was a law passed by the federal government - The Americans with Disabilities Act (ADA). The law essentially made it unlawful for any business, open to the public, to treat a person with a disability any different than they treated an abled bodied.

In other words, if a business was open to the public and abled bodied persons could park in the parking lot, enter into the business, enjoy it's goods and services, including using the restroom facilities, then a person in a wheelchair should be able to do the same and not be excluded from the facility because there was no place to accommodate persons in wheelchairs.

This law became the law of the land in 1990. There was thousands of business that didn't come close to being in compliance. They had no restroom facilities with grab bars for people in wheelchairs to use to help them use the restroom. There was no designated parking for disable persons to park their car and safely remove themselves and enter into the premise and seating inside the business almost never was sufficient to accommodate persons in wheelchairs.

This new law covered professional service providers like doctors and lawyers, government buildings, restaurants and just about every place open to the public. Buildings, unless they were specifically excluded by law, also were required to have operating elevators, in addition to stairs,in order to accommodate wheelchair, bound and other disabled persons to enter their premises to obtain services.

I became aware of this law because my mother-in-law had an appointment to go to her doctor's office. She was in a wheelchair.

While there she had to use the restroom. They told her there was no restroom for her to use on that floor and in order to use the restroom she had to go downstairs. She was in a wheelchair. How was she to get downstairs by herself?

In addition, it was determined that the restroom downstairs did not have grab bars that she could use to lift herself from the wheelchair and use the restroom by herself. She was unable to use the restroom in a timely manner and she soiled herself.

This was very upsetting to her and to me as well. I researched for an answer and found out about, at that time, the new Americans with Disabilities Act (ADA) law. I sued the owners and applied the law. The case was won. I then realized there were thousands of disabled persons who were in the same position as my mother-in-law. I represented a few of them and the word got out about my new practice discipline.

Hundreds of new clients began to call on my office for assistance. I represented them in droves and the local business establishments, chambers of commerce, and business associations created an uproar about the number of lawsuits being filed against the so called "unprotected small businesses" being preyed upon by malicious lawsuits filed by a renegade attorney.

While other lawyers were doing the same, I was nevertheless, singled out by the news media and even area politicians. Ultimately, even the State Bar received a complaint that I was doing something illegal. Even some judges did not like what I was doing. In effect, like the lady in the biblical story caught in adultery, I was brought before authorities to be "stoned", in a sense.

However, I reminded the courts, the news media, and all involved that this was the law. I did not make the law. The federal government did. I was enforcing the law on behalf of clients that for too long had been denied equal access. I then put forth the philosophy that each of them should put themselves or perhaps a loved one in the same position as my wheelchair clients who were being denied their civil rights and unable to have access as the law required.

In addition, there was a case where one of the business owners that was part of the complaining group was, unfortunately, involved in an accident. That accident put him in a position where he had to use a wheelchair. It was then that he suddenly realized that he could not access his own business because he was now wheelchair bound.

That same business owner apologized for the manner in which he had perceived the law and its application. It started a number of others to view it the same way. It took the same logic that Jesus used in the case of the adulterous woman in order to direct the attention to where it should have been –getting businesses not in compliance with the law to comply with the law.

Fortunately, after investigation and lots of controversy, I was cleared of any wrongdoing and continued to practice law on behalf of people with disabilities.

It was my faith in God that brought me through. I then took an interest in finding out the ways that the Bible might address how to be a better negotiator. I found it to be rich with examples and guidelines for conflict resolution and for reaching compromise where the parties can all win.

I do not write this chapter to try and convert you or any reader to believe the way I do. However, the Biblical concepts within this chapter are powerful and effective and many of the tried and true negotiation tactics and techniques used throughout the world have the same foundation and principles.

As a student of the Bible and its words, wisdom, and truth I have used God's word in many negotiations and it has never guided me wrong.

You don't have to be a believer in order for God's wisdom and word to work. It is simply based on a system that has worked in the past, works in the present and will continued to do so in the future to come. If you want to be a power negotiator learn these concepts.

The Power of Words:

For bad:

The tongue also is a fire, a world of evil among the parts of the body. It corrupts the whole person, sets the whole course of his life on fire, and is itself set on fire by hell. But no man can tame the tongue. It is a restless evil, full of deadly poison (James 3:6, 8). Always remember, what you hear or are told during a negotiation should always be viewed with caution and circumspect. Human beings lie to get their way. Test what is said with facts.

With his mouth the godless man destroys his neighbor (Proverbs 11:9).

The words of a gossip are like choice morsels, they go down to a man's inmost parts (Proverbs 18:8).People love gossip and negotiations are often tainted with it. Beware of gossip and do your best to verify things you are told. Most importantly, don't engage in gossip yourself. It will affect your ability to negotiate successfully.

Words are very powerful tools and can make or break negotiations. Being mindful of the words we speak before we voice them is a trait that successful negotiators are well aware of. Therefore, we should think before we speak because one ill spoken word can start a consuming fire that will burn down all of the building blocks set up to support a successful negotiation.

For good:

A word aptly spoken is like apples of gold in settings of silver (Proverbs 25:11). Words are powerful. Use words to communicate empathy to the other side. Let them know you understand their position. It breaks down barriers and opens up the door to honest and effective communication.

Pleasant words are a honeycomb, sweet to the soul and healing to the bones (Proverbs 16:24). This proverb is like the Feel, Felt, Found tactic. During negotiations, appreciate and recognize how the other side feels and then show another view that helps them get what they want and also gives you what you need as well.

The tongue of the righteous is choice silver, but the heart of the wicked is of little value. The lips of the righteous nourish many, but fools die for lack of judgment (Proverbs 10: 20, 21).

The tongue is a powerful weapon. It evokes joy, creates pain, sooths hurt feelings and destroys or restores relationships.

Reckless words pierce like a sword, but the tongue of the wise brings healing (Proverbs 12:18).

The tongue that brings healing is a tree of life, but a deceitful tongue crushes the spirit (Proverbs 15:4).

The tongue has the power of life and death (Proverbs 18:21). Using words can build, heal or steal. It literally has the power of life and death not only in a spiritual way but the way one's life can be affected and whether success comes or destruction abounds.

One of the words you should use very sparingly when negotiating is "why". The word why initself is not a bad word. However, the way it is often applied during negotiations sends the receiver of the question an unconscious challenge.

Why places pressure upon the receiver to explain himself or herself or to justify their position either of which can create problems in negotiation.

Use words like "how" or "what" in a question manner instead of why. This makes the negotiation opponent feel he or she is in control and fosters the likelihood that you can get more information that would answer your why question anyway. It also opens up more avenues to use the information gained from the questions to help seal the deal.

Listen before you respond:

He who answers before listening-that is his folly and his shame (Proverbs 18:13).

Do you see a man who speaks in haste? There is more hope for a fool than for him (Proverbs 29:20).

Everyone should be quick to listen, slow to speak and slow to become angry (James 1:19).

There is an old saying that the reason people have two ears and one mouth is because we should listen twice as much as we talk. That is so true when we are engaged in negotiating.

Learn to listen and listen well. Engaged listening will provide you with the information you need to make the next move or form the next phrase that you need to use in order to help the negotiations along the way.

There is a difference in listening and hearing. It's easy to hear what someone is saying but it takes effort to listen to what they are saying. If you are only hearing you are not listening and will almost always miss something that is important to the other person in the negotiating process. How will you know what the important parts are if you are only hearing and not truly listening?

In negotiations, too often, the one not talking is hearing what is being said but is so engaged in formulating a response or is only waiting to make his or her next point, that the information being provided by the one speaking is lost.

Think about it, have you ever been engaged in a conversation with someone and you want to make sure you get your point across? They are talking to you and you're hearing them, but if you had to repeat the main points of what they just said you couldn't do it because you missed most of it thinking about what you are getting ready to say as soon as they stop talking.

Once the other side stops then you make your point. However, the response you get is nothing but a blank stare and then a question "didn't you hear what I just said?" The question really should be "did you listen to what I just said?"

When we truly listen there are great benefits that arise from it. First, if you are engaged in really listening, the person you are talking to or negotiating with can pick up on it right away. They do this through your body language like the nodding of your head, your eye contact and even a verbal cue like you saying, "I understand" or "I see." This shows respect, interest in what they are saying, and gives them a feeling of importance. Whether you agree with them is not the issue. The issue is they feel they are getting across to you and that opens them up to being receptive to what you are saying as well.

The Bible counsels us to listen first and never speak in haste. This tactic along will set you apart from most negotiators as it provides the ability for you to appear to be calm and in control and to obtain vital information that you might otherwise not get when you aren't truly listening.

Don't Talk Too Much

When words are many, sin is not absent, but he who holds his tongue is wise (Proverbs 10:19).

A man of knowledge uses words with restraint, and a man of understanding is even-tempered (Proverbs 17:27).

A fool finds no pleasure in understanding but delights in airing his own opinions (Proverbs 18:2).

Even a fool is thought wise if he keeps silent, and discerning if he holds his tongue (Proverbs 17:28).

A man of understanding holds his tongue (Proverbs 11:12).

The Bible teaches silence as a powerful tool in dealing with relations between people. Talking too much has derailed many negotiations that could have otherwise ended successfully.

There is a quote that is often attributed to Abraham Lincoln and Mark Twain wherein they said words to the effect. "Better to remain silent and be thought a fool than to speak out and remove all doubt." There is much controversy as to whether Lincoln ever actually created this quote. Nevertheless, it's genesis is consistent with what the Bible says about keeping silent in appropriate circumstances.

Silence is the one powerful tool that is often never used during negotiations. Rather, as the Bible points out when there are many words spoken mistakes (sin) abound and can creep in and destroy what one is trying to accomplish. (Proverbs 10:19). In fact, it is foolish to be opinionated and not be open to the other side's position. (Proverbs 18:12). Being silent at the appropriate time makes you appear wise and keeps the other side on their toes wondering. This automatically gives you an opportunity to be a better negotiator.

Weigh Your Words: Think Before You Speak

The heart of the righteous weighs its answers, but the mouth of the wicked gushes evil (Proverbs 15:28).

He who guards his lips guards his life, but he who speaks rashly will come to ruin (Proverbs 13:3).

He who guards his mouth and his tongue keeps himself from calamity (Proverbs 21:23).

It's just as important to know what to say when you do speak in negotiations as it is to be silent in negotiations at the right time. The two tactics used together are extremely powerful to persuade and dissuade.

Make Your Words Timely and Appropriate.

A man finds joy in giving an apt reply—and how good is a timely word! (Proverbs 15:23)

A gentle answer turns away wrath, but a harsh word stirs up anger (Proverbs 15:1).

Speak The Truth

Keep your tongue from evil and your lips from speaking lies (Psalm 34:13).

A false witness will not go unpunished, and he who pours out lies will not go free (Proverbs 19:5, 9).

The Lord detests lying lips, but he delights in men who are truthful (Proverbs 12:22).

The one thing I learned early on in my negotiating career is that truth should always be spoken. Don't deviate from it. Tell it like it is. Lying or stretching the truth will only hurt your negotiating efforts and can be very costly. During my litigation career, even in trial, I looked at the trial process as a negotiation. There are two sides to a trial. If it's a civil lawsuit then the plaintiff is seeking to negotiate with the jury, using the facts and testimony, to get a favorable conclusion. The defendant is doing just the opposite.

Both sides present their cases. They are negotiating with the jury. Truth is very important during this negotiation. During trial, I would always seek to get the truth out of the defendant and show that he or she or in the case of a company, was not truthful. I did this through a process called cross examination. I would deliberately ask questions on crucial points that I already knew the answer too and get the defendant to say something different.

Usually, the defendant had already answered the question, at some point before the trial, in a different way under oath either in what is known as a deposition that was taken under oath or had already answered the question differently under oath in the current trial.

When the defendant answered contrary to his or her prior testimony under oath, I would point it out so the jury could clearly see the defendant was not telling the truth. Oftentimes I would ask the question different ways in order to make sure the jury got the point and that I was not using any tricks against the defendant.

Once it was clearly shown that the defendant was lying, the credibility of the defendant and any defense that was being put forth was severely damaged. On these occasions the verdict in my client's favor hinged on the untruthful information. Juror's afterwards would state later that the untruthfulness was the key point to them in reaching their verdict.

It doesn't matter if it's in the courtroom, the boardroom or in your room, the truth matters when negotiating with people.

Use Words That Edify

The tongue that brings healing is a tree of life, but a deceitful tongue crushes the spirit (Proverbs 15:4).

Pleasant words are a honeycomb, sweet to the soul and healing to the bones (Proverbs 16:24).

An anxious heart weighs a man down, but a kind word cheers him up (Proverbs 12:25).

Let us therefore make every effort to do what leads to peace and to mutual edification (Romans 14:19).

Therefore encourage one another and build each other up (1 Thessalonians 5:11)

Remember, negotiation is the art of bargaining with others in order to complete a business transaction or to get into agreement with someone that is important to us. I have learned that biblical principles protect one from crossing the line between good techniques and tactics and wrongful manipulation.

One of the principles that the bible supports is not to worry about the outcome after you've done all you can do. Worrying won't help one bit. Develop the mindset during negotiation that once you've done the best you can do and it appears that it's not going to work, simply walk away.

Of course you want to make the deal. However, if you want it too badly, you will have given up your bargaining power. You will be subject to just caving in to get a deal and that usually is a bad result. Jesus taught, "Therefore do not worry about tomorrow, for tomorrow will worry about itself." (Matthew 6:34 NIV).

If you give a person everything they want, you will probably land the deal. But in reality what have you landed? You have no power. But, when you are willing to walk away, and the other side knows it, you have power and the ability to extract what you or your client needs.

When negotiating, always know the bottom line and what you are not willing to take as much as what you are willing to take. If you get to the point where the negotiations clearly are not progressing the way you want them to the power to walk away should be exercised.

When you do walk away, it should be in a manner that sends a message that the door may still be open if the other side decides to reconsider and wants to come back to discuss terms more favorable.

Don't Waste Time

Psalm 90:12 instructs us to make the most of our time. It talks about the fact that human existence is very short and we should take note of that fact and make sure we number our days and apply them to wisdom – to make the best use of our time without wasting any.

One implication of this point is to avoid wasting time in negotiation. Make every moment count. Don't waste time entertaining things that aren't important and aren't conducive to getting to a conclusion that provides you with what you or your client wants.

One example of this concept is where money is involved and there is not a substantial gap between what one side wants and what the other side is willing to pay. In such circumstances, there should be a cost benefit analysis done on the spot. If this issue is going to be a sticking point that takes more than time and effort than what it's worth in terms of the overall negotiation, its best to accept less and move on. Don't waste time on issues that will overall cost more than what they are worth.

Key Points To Remember

- Use the Bible to negotiate like Jesus. The system works whether you believe in Him or not.
- Use the power of words from a biblical standpoint.
- Listen before you respond
- Don't talk too much
- Always speak the truth
- Don't waste time
- Walk away when negotiations leave you no choice rather than just accepting any deal.
- The Bible and Jesus' methodology are good guidelines to follow for successful negotiations
- Words have power. Use them wisely
- Think before you speak
- Listen more than you talk
- Always tell the truth

Chapter Seventeen

If It's Not Enough, Don't be Afraid to Ask for More.

Once people make up their mind about something, it's extremely hard for them to back off the decision. They've made a commitment. It's just human nature to want to stick to the decision and logically follow through. In the book, Influence by Robert Caldini, referenced earlier in this book, this concept is described as one of the six powerful ways to influence people. It's the power of commitment.

When negotiating you can use this concept to get even more out of the process. In negotiation circles it's referred to as "nibbling." The nibbling tactic is used to get small concessions that at the moment don't seem that important in terms of the big picture, but once agreed to and looked at overall, nibbling is huge and can make the difference in getting what you want or not.

Think about it for a moment. Picture in your mind a small mouse and a large chunk of cheese. The cheese does not disappear all at once. The little mouse is nibbling. Small bites little by little and before you know it the entire chunk of cheese is consumed and gone.

This happens in negotiations all the time between individuals, family members, organizations, companies, governments and countries. A little concession here and there is the grease that keeps the gears oiled to get where you want to go.

Car dealerships use the nibbling concept very effectively. They teach their salespeople to assist in first getting you to make a decision about a car and make a commitment that you want it. Once you make the decision to buy it your resistance is down. In your mind you've accomplished your purpose. It's then the nibbling starts. The car salesperson starts to talk about all of the accessories that can be added to the car that the model you just choice doesn't have.

However, for just a little more cost, that marvelous accessory can be added. This tactic is used often even if you've thought the process through and decided on a car that had accessories you felt you wanted. There are always additions that can be added to the car, like extended warranty, special tinted windows and etc.

Once you are in the car dealership closing room and the nibbling starts, anything that is added is where the car dealership makes it profit. The first objective was to get you to decide on a car and make that commitment. If you've ever purchased a car or been with someone while they went through the purchase process this scene is likely very familiar with you.

Some of the best nibblers in the world are children. If you have children or grandchildren you've been a victim of this negotiation technique time and time again and likely didn't even see it coming or realize what had happened. Children are natural negotiators and they are extremely good at it. They don't learn those skills at school. It's part of their natural born makeup. Everything a child gets that he/she wants, beyond the obvious things parents and love ones give them, is usually through some form of negotiation.

I have a granddaughter and she is one of the best negotiators I know. To her I am Papa and she knows that she can get just about anything out of me that she wants, despite the fact that I've made promises to myself time and time again that I would be on guard and not do things to spoil her.

She knows instinctively that she won't get everything she wants from me if she just asks outright, so she has become a ninja nibbler with her Papa.

I am an avid reader of books and purchase them on a consistent basic online and offline. She has picked up that trait as well and we often shop together in Barnes and Noble's bookstore. Inside that store is a children's area where they also have toys and other items for children as well as books and learning materials. She knows I'm a sucker for buying her books to read to enhance her knowledge. She also knows there is a toy section inside the store.

Her nibble tactic was used brilliantly on one occasion where I agreed to take her to Barnes and Noble to look for a set of books she wanted. I had also said to her I would only buy the books and nothing else. She looked at me and smiled. We arrived at the bookstore and found the books she wanted. I agreed to purchase them. She was so happy and gushing and hugging me and then smoothly asked if she could take a look at a Lego building set that caught her eye. I said "yes, but we aren't going to buy it." She said nothing and moved to the area where the Lego toys were.

She found a Lego set and looked at it and starting talking about how this would fit with her other Lego sets and how she could learn so much from building this set and how we could have so much fun building it together. Then she looked at me and said "Papa can I have this too? We can build it together and I will learn more from it." She knew how to present the nibble.

She knows I am a sucker for doing anything that will help her learn constructive things and, even more, she knows I will drop just about anything to spend time with her and do things together. What do you think happened? Yep, you're right. I bought the Lego set for her as well. She used the nibble tactic to get what she wanted.

Had she asked for all of that up front, the answer would likely have been no since I had already made the decision to purchase only the book set and I had told her that.

What's demonstrated here is that a person's mind always works to reinforce decisions that it has made. Power negotiators know how this works and use it to get the other side to agree to something that he or she wouldn't have agreed to earlier in the negotiation.

In my coaching and teaching of negotiations tactics I illustrate the power of nibbling by using what I call the "little hinge" technique. There is a saying that "little hinges opens big doors." In teaching this technique I ask the person or persons I am coaching to look at any door in the room. I tell them look how big that door is.

Now imagine that on the other side of that door is everything you want or need. You just have to go through that door to get it. However, you cannot open the door until you push or pull it forward and open it. I then remind them that the door won't function unless the "little hinges" that hold it up are engaged and allow the door to swing open. Therefore the concept of "little hinges open big doors." The ultimate goal is to move the door but it won't happen without the little hinges.

The ultimate goal in negotiations is to get what you want, but you must recognize that there are small things, like little concessions, small words or phrases, small gestures and body languages that lead the way to get what you want. Finally, after you've gotten the agreement complete, it's the little things beyond that that can close the door and seal the deal completely for what you want. "Little hinges open big doors."

In negotiations, always remember, you don't necessarily ask for everything up front. You wait for a moment of agreement in the negotiations, then go back, and "nibble" for a little extra.

Get the other side to commit to something significant first. People feel good after they have made the initial agreement. They feel a sense of relief that the tension and stress are over. It's at this point their mind is ready to reinforce the decision that they've just made. They are more open then to suggestions you may have. Knowing this you can put something you want to get accomplished in the negotiation. If at first you don't get it, always go back at the end of the negotiation to make another effort to get what you could not get earlier.

Be aware that the nibbling tactic works both ways. People will nibble on you as well. Just when you think the negotiations are over the nibbling comes. I've seen this happen countless times during negotiations when I've represented sellers in a real estate transaction.

The seller's main motivation is to always get the property sold at a price that meets their objective. Once this is accomplished and escrow is ready to be opened to close the deal, the seller feels a sense of accomplishment, the pressure and tension of the negotiations have drained away. As the buyer is ready to open escrow and deposit the check, he asks, "I assume you won't have a problem extending the close of escrow an additional 30 days?" The initial agreement was to close the escrow and transfer the property within 30 days. The nibble is for an additional 30 days.

At this point the seller is in a vulnerable position for two reasons. One, the seller has just made a sale, and feeling good about it. When the feeling exists, there is a tendency to give things away that you otherwise wouldn't. Secondly, and more likely, the seller is thinking, "Oh, oh I thought I had a sale and this thing was wrapped up. I don't want to take a chance on going back to negotiate for additional terms or get something more for an additional 30 days. If I do that, this whole deal might fall through. After all it's only an additional 30 days. I can wait for that." Often, you're at your most vulnerable position when the other person has made the decision to go ahead and then asks for additional "small concessions." Watch out for this nibbling tactic.

Look out for people nibbling on you and using the "little hinge" technique. The way you counter the nibble is to gently make the other person feel cheap or they are somehow acting unfairly or unethical. You must be careful with this because it could backfire on you. You could say with as much empathy as possible, "I understand, but I've reduced the price even below what I think I should be getting so I could help you out and close the deal, don't make me wait for the money too. Fair enough?"

Of course, you do this with as sincere a smile as possible and then just be silent. The point I want to make is you never just accept the nibble from the other side to get more out of you unless what you are giving has less value than the overall results you've accomplished in the negotiation at that point.

Key Points To Remember

- With a well-timed nibble, you can get things at the end of a negotiation that you couldn't have gotten the other side to agree to earlier.
- Set aside a point that's been a sticking point in earlier negotiations. This point can be brought up as a nibble later when the other side has made some major commitment and is ready to close the deal.
- Be prepared for the possibility that the nibbling tactic will be used on you at the last moment.
- When the other person nibbles on you, respond by making him or her feel cheap in a good-natured way.

Chapter Eighteen

Getting the Deal on Paper. Beware of the Pitfalls

Negotiating between friends, family and simple situations during one's day to day transactions are almost never reduced to writing. It's just a give and take and understanding that is usually lived up to between the people we know, like and trust.

However, in a more formal situation, what has been negotiated between parties should always be reduced to writing. Most people think of negotiating as just the verbal back and forth that takes place between people seeking to obtain their different wants and needs. Of course, that is the heart of any negotiation but, without something in writing to memorialize the points agreed upon it can become a horror story later on when someone claims that points that were negotiated are not recalled the same as one side or the other remembers.

As a skilled negotiator you must make it part of the negotiations that agreements are reduced to writing. It does not mean that disagreements won't come up later on about how the agreement should be enforced, but what it does do is make a record for what was agreed to so that it can be brought to the attention to both sides if heated disagreements occur or worse yet, the matter ends up in a courtroom to enforce the agreement.

From a negotiation standpoint here are some things that should be considered and put in to place, where possible after verbal agreements have been reached.

Don't Let the Other Side Write the Contract

In a typical negotiation, you verbally negotiate the details then put it into writing later for both parties to review and approve. Too often, I've found that any agreement prepared by the other side failed to cover every detail that was verbally agreed to. There are always points that are overlooked when verbally negotiating that must be detailed in writing and then the other sidehas to approve or negotiate the points when itstime to sit down to sign the written agreement.

That's when the side that writes the contract has a tremendous advantage over the side that doesn't. Chances are that the person writing the agreement will think of at least half-dozen things that did not come up during the verbal negotiations. That person can then write the clarification of that point to his or her advantage, leaving the other side to negotiate a change in the agreement when asked to sign it.

Don't let the other side write the contract because it puts you at a disadvantage. This applies to brief counter proposals just as much as it does to agreements that are hundreds of pages long. For example, a real estate agent may present an offer to purchase a commercial building on behalf of a represented buyer for the sum of $10,000,000 in price with additional terms and conditions as well.

The seller agrees to the general terms of the offer, but wants the price to be $200,000 higher. At this point either the seller's agent or the buyer's agent can write up additional offers, sometimes referred to as counteroffers. The seller's agent could simply make a counteroffer that says "offer accepted as to all terms and conditions, except the price shall be $10,200,000."

If the buyer's agent writes up the counteroffer, after having verbal discussions with the seller's agent, the buyer's counteroffer could be presented as "counteroffer accepted in the amount of $10,200,000, except that additional $200,000 to be carried back as a second mortgage all due and payable within 3 years from the date of the close of escrow with 3% interest annual accrual. This counteroffer is to be accepted within 48 hours."

Here it can be seen that the sum of $10,200,000 is clearly agreed between buyer and seller to be the price of the commercial building. However, depending on who is writing the offer or counteroffer the details may be viewed entirely different by one party or the other.

If the person who writes a one-paragraph counter-offer can affect it so much, think how much that person could affect a multi-page contract. Remember, this may not just be a matter of taking advantage of the other side. Both sides may genuinely think that they had reached agreement on a point whereas their interpretations may be substantially different when they write it out.

If you are to be the one writing the contract, it's a good idea to keep notes throughout the negotiation and put a check mark in the margin against any point that will be part of the final agreement. This will remind you to include all the points that you wanted. In addition, when you write the contract, you may be reluctant to include a point of agreement unless you can specifically recall the other side agreeing to it.

Your notes will give you the confidence to include it even if you don't remember it clearly. If you have other people on your side involved in the negotiation, be sure to have all of them review the contract before you present it to the other side. You may have overlooked a point that you should have included or you may have misinterpreted a point.

In our litigious society there isn't much point in making an agreement that won't hold up in court. However, it's a good idea to have the agreement approved by your attorney before you have it signed. In a complicated agreement what you prepare and have the other side sign may be no more than a letter of intent. Have your attorney work on it later to make it a legal document. It's better that you devote your energy to reaching agreement.

If you have prepared an agreement that you think the other side may be reluctant to sign, it's a good idea to put language in the agreement like "Subject to your attorney's approval," to encourage them to sign it. Once the verbal negotiations are over, get a memorandum of agreement signed as quickly as possible. The longer you give them before they see it in writing the greater the chances that they'll forget what they agreed to and question what you've prepared.

Also, make sure they understand the agreement. Don't be tempted to have them sign something when you know they're not clear on the implications. If they don't understand and something goes wrong they will always blame you. They will never accept responsibility.

In fact, there is a concept within the jurisprudence of the law and generally accepted by the courts that terms within a written document will be enforced more strictly against the one who prepared the document than against the one who didn't. The rationale behind this is the person who prepared the document is the one that was in the best position to know and understand what the terms and conditions mean within the document and should have gotten it right in the first place.

Therefore, while its highly recommended that you as a negotiator be the one to create the document, you must be careful to make sure it reflects accurately the things that were truly agreed to and you are prepared to back them up in court, if necessary. Otherwise, it could be the court that will interpret the contract against you and in favor of the opposing party.

I find it helpful to write out a best and worst-case scenario before I go into negotiations. This is not something you would share with the other side, but it is helpful for comparison between what you expected to accomplish to what you actually ended up with at the conclusion of the negotiation.

Unless you have clearly established the best and worst-case scenario you could expect from the negotiations before you begin you may end up with a deal that is less than satisfactory.

As an effective and complete negotiator, you should always try to be the one that writes the contract. When the verbal negotiations are over, it's time for someone to put everything in writing and the person who gets to put it in writing has definite power in the negotiations. There are bound to be little details that you didn't think of when you were verbally negotiating that need to be specified in the written contract.

If you're the one who gets to write the contract, you can write those to your favor. Then it's up to the other person to negotiate them out when it comes to signing the contract. So, try to be the one who writes the contract, even if you have to pay an experienced attorney to do it for you. It's a good investment in the long run.

You should also read the agreement every time there is a change made. It may be tedious and time consuming to do so. Nevertheless, do it. Here's the danger if you don't.

Let's say you're busy and you feel comfortable with the minor changes that the other side has agreed to make and they make some changes and send them to you. When the revised version comes across your desk, you quickly review the area where the changes are supposed to be and it appears the changes have been made. You then turn to the back page and sign off on the agreement.

Unfortunately, because you didn't take the time to reread the entire contract you didn't realize that they had also changed something else. It could be something as significant as making a change in the interest rate on a mortgage contract or as minor as making a payment due date on the 4th instead of the 5th, either of which you don't discovery until years later when something goes wrong and you need to enforce the contract. By then, you may not even remember what you agreed to, and you can only assume that because you signed it you must have agreed to it.

Yes, you may have a wonderful lawsuit with a claim that the other side defrauded you-but why expose yourself to that kind of trouble. It could have all been avoided had you reread the contract all the way through every time it came across your desk for your signature.

People Believe What They See In Writing

The printed word has great power over people. Most people believe what they see in writing, even if they won't believe it when they just hear about it.

Many years ago, there was a T.V. show called "Candid Camera." It was hosted by Allen Fount and they pulled various pranks on the show to show in reality how people in general react to certain things. On one episode it was shown how Candid Camera closed the whole state of Delaware down.

Allen Font, the host of the show, dressed in an "official-looking uniform and hat" held a clipboard and stood at a barricade with a sign overhead on the freeway saying, "DELAWARE CLOSED TODAY."

People heading into Delaware from the state of Pennsylvania were told they couldn't get in. Amazingly, people fell for it. One woman even asked if New Jersey was closed and said she would go there instead. One person asked "how long will it be closed, my wife and kids are inside." This story is all over the internet with videos and etc. if you want to check it out for yourself.

My point in mentioning it in this chapter is to simply point out that people are very susceptible to believing what they see in writing.

People believe what they see in writing. Human beings are more visually influenced than by any other of the human senses that we use to interpret and communicate within our environment and by which we make ultimate decisions.

That's why I'm such a big believer in written and visual presentations using presentation binders, PowerPoint and other visuals during negotiations, training or sales sessions.

When someone is exposed to you making a presentation in writing or visually that says who you are, what you stand for and what value you provide to solve the problems they are facing, along with testimonials you become believable. Recognize this when you're negotiating with people.

We live in a sue happy society so it's very important to get things down in writing even if nothing ever comes up that will test the agreement from a legal standpoint. In fact, from a prudent negotiators standpoint, if the other side is reluctant to sign a document that fairly reflects what the verbal agreement is that's a sure sign that somethingis wrong and further negotiations need to be had to clarify some points or perhaps there should not be a negotiated deal at all.

Successful negotiators know that it's important to get the final verbal agreement in writing. So every chance you get put things in writing. Take the time during the verbal negotiations to say, "Let me be sure that I understand what you're proposing." Then stop to write down your understanding of the point that you were discussing.

Show it to the other side, but you don't have to have them sign it at this point. All you're doing is getting them used to seeing it in writing. This subliminally confirms what, up to that point, has only been a verbal understanding. If you do this at intervals during the discussion, you'll have much less trouble getting them to sign the final written contract.

It's important to realize that at every point of the negotiation, the other side is more persuaded by what they see in writing.

What's the bottom line?

Because people don't question what they see in writing, you should always present written backup evidence to support your proposal. If the negotiation includes expectations that the other side will meet certain requirements it also helps to confirm those requirements in writing.

The transition from a verbal negotiation to a written contract can be a delicate one, but successful negotiators know how to set it up so that it doesn't become a traumatic experience.

Key Points To Remember

- Reduce the negotiated agreement to writing

- You prepare the written agreement if possible, not the other side

- Remember, people believe what they see in writing. If it's in writing the more credibility it will have.

- Always back up your proposals with written evidence.

Chapter Nineteen

Negotiation Review Guidelines

In this final chapter I point out some crucial steps that should be followed in every negotiation. They are fundamental and if mastered will help you become a very good negotiator whether you negotiate on behalf of yourself or on behalf of others.

There are fifteen(15)basic steps that underline good negotiation. Make them a habit and you will know the secret of How To Negotiate To Get What You Want and you can become a Power Negotiator.

1. Prepare, prepare, prepare. Enter a negotiation without proper preparation and you've already lost. Start with yourself. Make sure you are clear on what you really want out of the arrangement. Research the other side to better understand their needs as well as their strengths and weaknesses. Enlist help from experts, such as an accountant, attorney or tech guru if needed

2. Get the Other Side to Commit First

Power Negotiators know that you're usually better off if you can get the other side to commit to a position first. Several reasons are obvious:

- Their first offer may be much better than you expected.

- It gives you information about them before you have to tell them anything.

- It enables you to bracket their proposal. If they state a price first, you can bracket them, so if you end up splitting the difference, you'll get what you want. If they can get you to commit first, they can then bracket your proposal. Then if you end up splitting the difference, they get what they want.

The less you know about the other side or the proposition that you're negotiating, the more important the principle of not going first becomes.

3. Act Dumb, Not Smart

To Power Negotiators, smart is dumb and dumb is smart. When you are negotiating, you're better off acting as if you know less than everybody else does, not more. The dumber you act, the better off you are unless your apparent I.Q. sinks to a point where you lack any credibility.

There is a good reason for this. With a few rare exceptions, human beings tend to help people they see as less intelligent or informed rather than taking advantage of them. Of course, there are a few ruthless people out there who will try to take advantage of weak people, but most people want to compete with people they see as brighter and help people they see as less bright.

So, the reason for acting dumb is that it diffuses the competitive spirit of the other side. How can you fight with someone who is asking you to help them negotiate with you? How can you carry on any type of competitive banter with a person who says, "I don't know, what do you think?" Most people, when faced with this situation, feel sorry for the other person and go out of their way to help him or her.

There used to be a popular TV show named Columbo? Peter Falk, the actor, played a police detective who walked around in an old raincoat and a mental fog, chewing on an old cigar butt. He constantly wore an expression that suggested he had just misplaced something and couldn't remember what it was, let alone where he had left it. In fact, his success was directly attributable to how smart he was-by acting dumb. His demeanor was so disarming that the murderers came close to wanting him to solve his cases because he appeared to be so helpless.

The negotiators who let their egos take control of them and come across as sharp, sophisticated negotiators commit to several things that work against them in a negotiation. These include being the following:

- A fast decision-maker who doesn't need time to think things over.

- Someone who would not have to check with anyone else before going ahead.

- Someone who doesn't have to consult with experts before committing.

- Someone who would never stoop to pleading for a concession.

- Someone who would never be overridden by a supervisor.

- Someone who doesn't have to keep extensive notes about the progress of the negotiation and refer to them frequently.

The Power Negotiator who understands the importance of acting dumb retains these options:

- Requesting time to think it over so that he or she can thoroughly think through the dangers of accepting or the opportunities that making additional demands might bring.

- Deferring a decision while he or she checks with a committee or board of directors.

- Asking for time to let legal or technical experts review the proposal.

- Pleading for additional concessions.

- Using Good Guy/Bad Guy to put pressure on the other side without confrontation.

- Taking time to think under the guise of reviewing notes about the negotiation.

I act dumb by asking for the definitions of words. If the other side uses a technical term or some big word I act like I don't have a clue what it means even if I do. I might say something like "I've heard that word or term before, but what does it mean can you please explain it to me?

It may be a cluster of numbers or a spreadsheet. The numbers may appear to be simple, but I will say "I'm sorry, I am just not getting it. I apologize, would you please go over those figures again?"

This makes them think: What a dunce I've got on my hands this time. In this way, I lay to rest the competitive spirit that could have made a compromise very difficult for me to accomplish. Now the other side stops fighting me and starts trying to help me.

Be careful that you're not acting dumb in your area of expertise. If you hold yourself out as an expert in a particular area, you would never want to show ignorance or play the dummy in that case. For example, if you are a building contractor, you don't scratch your head and ask that blueprints be explained to you.

Win-win negotiating depends on the willingness of each side to be truly empathetic to the other side's position. That's not going to happen if both sides continue to compete with each other. Power Negotiators know that acting dumb diffuses that competitive spirit and opens the door to win-win solutions.

4. Concentrate on the Issues

Power Negotiators know that they should always concentrate on the issues and not be distracted by the actions of the other negotiators. Have you ever watched tennis on television and seen a highly emotional star like John McEnroe jumping up and down at the other end of the court. You wonder to yourself, "How on Earth can anybody play tennis against somebody like that? It's such a game of concentration, it doesn't seem fair."

The answer is that good tennis players understand that only one thing affects the outcome of the game of tennis. That's the movement of the ball across the net. What the other player is doing doesn't affect the outcome of the game at all as long as you know what the ball is doing. So in that way, tennis players learn to concentrate on the ball, not on the other person.

When you're negotiating, the ball is the movement of the goal concessions across the negotiating table. It's the only thing that affects the outcome of the game, but it's so easy to be thrown off by what the other people are doing, isn't it?

To be an effective negotiator concentrate on the issues, not on the personalities. You should always be thinking, "Where are we now, compared to where we were an hour ago or yesterday or last week?" Keeping your eye on the ball to make sure it's going in the direction you want is always the goal in negotiations. Otherwise, it is likely to become a losing situation.

5. Use Silence As A Major Negotiation Tactic

Recall in earlier chapters in this book, I pointed out the power of silence as a negotiating tactic. It's very powerful when used at the right moment. Quite frankly, it is one of the most powerful, but least used negotiation tools. Train yourself to simply shut up after you've made a point or said something that makes it clear a response should be coming from the other side.

Silence will provide tremendous pressure for the other side to break it and say something. Often, the response will give you more information that you can use to help you in the negotiation process. Of course, if the other side is skilled and knows the power of silence it may, in rare, situations turn out to be a game of silence. In that case, you can simply repeat what you just said and wait for a response. This will usually get a response and you haven't lost anything by breaking the silence.

6. Anticipate compromise. You should expect to make concessions and plan what they might be. Of course, the other side is thinking the same, so never take their first offer. Even if it's better than you'd hoped for. Practice your best look of disappointment and politely decline. You never know what else you can get.

7. Pay attention to timing. Timing is important in any negotiation. Surely, you must know what to ask for. But be sensitive to *when* you ask for it. There are times to press ahead, and times to wait. When you are looking your best is the time to press for what you want. But beware of pushing too hard and poisoning any long-term relationship.

8. Leave your ego behind. The best negotiators either don't care or don't *show* they care about who gets credit for a successful deal. Their talent is in making the other side feel like the final agreement was all *their* idea.

9. Ramp up your listening skills. The best negotiators are often quiet listeners who patiently let others have the floor while they make their case. They never interrupt. Encourage the other side to talk first. That helps set up one of negotiation's oldest maxims: Whoever mentions numbers first, loses. While that's not always true, it's generally better to sit tight and let the other side go first. Even if they don't mention numbers, it gives you a chance to ask what they are thinking.

10. If you don't ask, you don't get. Another tenet of negotiating is "Go high or go home." As part of your preparation, define your highest *justifiable* price. If you can argue convincingly, don't be afraid to aim high. But no ultimatums, please. Take-it-or-leave-it offers are usually out of place.

11. Offer and expect commitment. The glue that keeps deals from unraveling is an unshakable commitment to deliver. You should offer this comfort level to others. Likewise, avoid deals where the other side does not demonstrate commitment.

12. Don't absorb their problems. In most negotiations, you will hear all the other side's problems and reasons they can't give you what you want. They want their problems to become yours, but don't let them.

Instead, deal with each as they come up and try to solve them. If their "budget" is too low, for example, maybe there are other places that money could come from.

13. Stick to your principles. As an individual and a business owner, you likely have a set of guiding principles — values that you just won't compromise. If you find negotiations crossing those boundaries, it might be a deal you can live without.

14. Close with confirmation. At the close of any meeting — even if no final deal is struck — recap the points covered and any areas of agreement. Make sure everyone confirms. Follow-up with appropriate letters or emails. Do not leave behind loose ends.

15. Always congratulate the other side

When you're through negotiating you should always congratulate the other side. However poorly you think the other person may have done in the negotiations, congratulate them. Say, "Wow! you did a fantastic job negotiating that. I realize that I didn't get as good a deal as I could have done, but frankly, it was worth it because I learned so much about negotiating. You were brilliant." You want the other person to feel that he or she won in the negotiations.

However, don't do this in a condescending way. You don't want to come off as offensive or in a manner that would ridicule the other side.

Never gloat and always congratulate.

Power Negotiators always want the other parties thinking that they won in the negotiations. It starts by asking for more than you expect to get. It continues through all the other tactics and techniques that are designed to service the perception that the other side is winning. It ends with congratulating the other side.

If you let these fifteen (15) principles guide your conduct when you're negotiating, they will serve you well and help you become a Power Negotiator.

Conclusion

This book was written from the heart. I've put the substance of my more than 40 years of experience in practicing law, sitting as a Judge Pro Tem hearing numerous court cases, representing buyers and sellers in real estate transactions, countless mediations and arbitrations, creating and operating several small businesses and expending thousands of dollars obtaining some of the best training in negotiation skills, business development and marketing to make it happen.

I sincerely hope that you will find a thought, some point, tactic or technique that will help you along the way to become a better negotiator, and more importantly, a better person dedicated to providing value to fellow human beings to help solve problems and remove the pain that is encountered by human beings every day, and who are struggling to make sense out of a cluttered and confused world.

My purpose on earth and the legacy I want to leave will, in part, be fulfilled if what I've written helps someone learn how to negotiate and get what they want and get to yes in a world that constantly says no.

About the Author

Roy Landers is a practicing attorney and president of his own Law Firm, the Landers Law Group, PC. He has practiced law for over 30 years and his practice emphasis has been in the area of business, taxation, civil rights, employment and real estate.

As a business attorney, he assists and coaches small business owners in business development, marketing, mergers and acquisitions, asset protection and business succession planning. He served as a Judge Pro Tem within the San Diego Judicial system and heard and ruled on numerous cases on a variety of small business issues.

He is an accomplished speaker and presenter and has presented numerous seminars on subjects such as lessons in leadership, the power of mindset, negotiation strategies and numerous other subjects. He is also available for keynote speaking.

His current concentration is business marketing strategies to obtain maximum results and providing copywriting services in several areas such as content creation and marketing, newsletter production, finance, business, email strategies and social media.

In addition, he counsels and represents veterans on obtaining veteran benefits, qualifying for service connected disabilities and processes appeals of benefit denials. As a disabled U.S. Navy veteran, he is very sensitive to the needs of veterans seeking benefits.

Roy's passion is helping others to better themselves and he strives to assist in self-development, acquisition of leadership skills and empowerment of others. He has a seminar series that he speaks and teaches on including but not limited to:

- Power, Passion and Prosperity
- How to negotiate for anything you want
- The art of influence and the magic of rapport
- How to overcome any fear or phobia
- Getting rid of excess baggage (The power of mindset)

He is a graduate of Thomas Jefferson School of Law where he earned his Juris Doctorate (JD) degree and the University of San Diego School of Law where he earned his Master of Law in Taxation (LLM).

One of Roy's passions is creating business opportunities and creating multiple streams of income for others. To that end he has developed several business models that any individual or business can replicate to maximize income and build a solid financial foundation.

His motto is: **Making a World of Difference Helping People To Prosper.** Get to know him at www.roylanders.com

To order additional copies of *How To Negotiation And Get What You Want*, please contact info@roylanders.com or by mail:

Roy Landers
Rainbow Publishing Company
10679 Westview Parkway
San Diego, CA 92126

www.ingramcontent.com/pod-product-compliance
Lightning Source LLC
Chambersburg PA
CBHW071546220526
45469CB00003B/943